# Corruption-The Inside Story

## 53 Capsules provided by

## Hugh G. Wetmore

# Corruption-The Inside Story

## 53 Capsules provided by

## Hugh G. Wetmore

**Text** © 2021 Hugh G. Wetmore
wetmore@singingtheword.co.za
**Publication** © 2021 Mbokodo Publishers
mbokodopublishers@gmail.com

### Disclaimer

**Corruption-The Inside Story**
ISBN-13: 978-1-990919-97-8 (paperback)

Typeset in 10/11 Adobe Garamond Pro by Mbokodo Publishers

**Take one Capsule a day to strengthen your Immunity to Corruption!**

# Preface

**By the author**

**Unless you're planning some fraud and corruption,
you will be glad you are reading this book**

Every day The News is reporting instances of Fraud and Corruption.

Our leaders often complain that Fraud and Corruption are endemic.

As early as 2012, Transparency International reports that 47% of South Africans paid a bribe that year. They ask you and me to "Fight Fraud and Corruption" - and we agree, yes - we want to.

But "HOW"? We need help, we need understanding of what we are up against, we need practical strategies to deal with these evils right in our own backyard.

We also need motivation. Because these evils are so common we can become cynical, Fraud & Corruption are so widespread, it seems society can't function without them, so we give up before we do anything about it. "What's the use?"

Read this book eagerly, as someone desperate for Hope.

It contains valuable information about Fraud and Corruption.

It re-kindles a motivational fire in you, to do something positive.

It supplies the fuel to keep that motivation burning, and it is hands-on practical.

# A Confession

As I write, I'm aware that I too struggle against the universal temptation to dishonesty. I am learning to know my personal weaknesses, the circumstances that lead me into temptation. No-one is immune, and the act of writing a book on Fraud and Corruption puts me in the moral firing line. On my back are the cross-hairs, the target. To fall is easy. So I must be extra careful. This book will hold me accountable.

Accountability is a good thing. Especially in the struggle for Integrity. By reading my book, you are holding me accountable to practice what I preach. Thank you!

~ Hugh G Wetmore

# Corruption- The Inside Story

**"Corruption costs South Africa R27 billion annually, and 76 000 jobs"**

No-one is proud of having a reputation for Corruption.

Yet every day there are people of all races, classes and background who are earning for themselves just such a reputation.

Efforts to curb Corruption by whistle blowing are good and necessary.

Honest citizens are exposing Corruption wherever they see it.

Yet instances of Corruption continue to multiply.

SO, HOW CAN WE CURB THE INCREASING CASES OF CORRUPTION?

What is needed is a Course of Capsules that will build up your immunity to Corruption.

That is the Course which this booklet offers - Capsules to strengthen your Immunity to the Temptation to be Corrupt.

Everyone is vulnerable to these Temptations to Corruption, because we are all Human.

So go ahead with a Commitment to Conquer Corruption **INSIDE,** in your own heart.

TAKE ONE CAPSULE A DAY ... ONE SHORT CHAPTER A DAY. Don't overdose by swallowing all the capsules at once!

# Part One

# The Faces of corruption and fraud

# Capsule 1 Examples of Fraud and Corruption

### Forged Certificates and Plagiarism

Theoretical Definitions are useful, but to hear of actual examples from real life will make these evils easier to understand and identify.

Each of these Examples will help us to recognise the Temptations that can infect us.

Then we can develop the Integrity that increases our resistance to these infections.

**Forged Certificates** "release into the job market people who simply cannot do what is required, and the whole community suffers. Service delivery creaks and the infrastructure crumbles. Knowledge is power, but a falsified certificate ultimately disempowers everyone" (W itness 19.1.09)

"More than 15% of all qualifications investigated by MIE Resource Services, the largest South African accreditation verification service, are bogus. A further 12% have been tampered with, usually in exaggerating symbols on matric certificates. Commonly, job-applicants jobs submit forged documentation while they are still studying" (Witness 8.7.02)

"Forty-seven teachers were fired by the Education Department for submitting fake qualifications. This will save the department about R1,2 million." (Witness 13.10.99)

"Zanele Kwawula (Mantshanhlola LP School, Pholela District) was sentenced to four years imprisonment for submitting a fake diploma to the Education Dept.." (Witness 16.9.99)

"Sixteen students from Edendale Hospital's nursing college were arrested on Tuesday for using bogus matric certificates." (Echo 27.7.2000)

In 2004 Sunday Times reporters bought three degrees, certified by the police as true copies of the originals, at internet cafes in Johannesburg and Pretoria - for a total of R730. At that price, anyone can afford to have a university degree!

"Fraudsters often present police with an altered forged original and a photocopy for certification. Many gullible employers have fallen victim to this ploy and end up giving work to people who ... have totally failed matric. Present labour legislation has made it extremely difficult to get rid of an unproductive employee even though he or she may have gained employment through submission of fraudulent documentation." (Witness 22.1.04)

**Plagiarism**

Plagiarism occurs when I present someone else's original work* as my own, without due acknowledgment of authors and sources. This is a serious offence because it amounts to intellectual fraud.

* "'Original work' includes published or unpublished documents, interpretations, computer software, designs, music, sounds, images, photographs, ideas or ideological frameworks obtained by working with another person or

in a group. The work can be published in print, or in the electronic media."

The Centre for Academic Integrity (USA) estimates that 70% of all students admit to dishonesty at one time or another. Rutgers University research matches this: "7 out of every 10 students has cheated, one of whom does it all the time". All South African Universities deal with allegations of this nature. Actions taken include: Expulsion, Suspension, Repeat the Course, Deducting marks, and other disciplinary measures. Many temptations come via the Internet, with its immense supply of quotable data. "Turnitin" is a web-based programme that can compare a student's work against a data-base of more than 4.5 billion pages obtained from the Internet, Newspapers, Journals, Books and other students' work. (W eekend W itness 14.7.07)

**How Do You Feel About These Examples? Admiration? Or Disgust?**

\*\*\*

# Capsule 2 More Examples: Theft, Licence And Customs Fraud, Sick Leave

## Theft

A Conveyancing Secretary Candida du Plessis, of a Pietermaritzburg legal firm frittered away R1.2 million of her employer's money on hand-outs to family, friends and needy people. She had other debts on her credit-card and on fashion-store-cards.

**https://www.iol.co.za/dailynews/news/law-firm-granted-sequestration-order-1300609**

Alan Gooderson when chairman of the National Hotel Association of SA, says that "theft of towels, face-cloths, sheets, bedspreads, Bibles, courtesy shampoo bottles and even television sets cost hoteliers millions. Some guests even strip the room of its curtains. The higher the star grading, the greater the theft." (Reader's Digest July 1994) Hotel guests are seldom among the poor. They come from the rich to middle classes. Gooderson's experience demolishes the theory that 'theft is caused by poverty'. Rather most theft is caused by Greed. This is why we must conquer Greed.

### Drivers' Licence Fraud

Learner's Licenses can be bought countrywide for as little as R20 , and are even accessible on the Internet. A number of syndicates sell licenses with the help of corrupt officials, An audit of 120 000 Limpopo drivers' licenses found 15 000 to have been issued illegally. (Witness 29.11.04). One in every eight drivers has a fraudulent license.

### Customs Fraud

The first conviction under the 'Proceeds of Crime Act 1997' was made when an order confiscating R1 million worth of ill-gotten gains from Jamnalall and Prashan Bantho. They defrauded Customs of about half the duty, and the VAT, payable on imported second hand clothing, by claiming it was destined for Swaziland. It was driven to a fronting address in Swaziland, but not unloaded. The delivery was finally made to the Bantho's Durban shop. (Natal Witness 20.7.1999)

**Sick Leave**

Many employees regard sick leave as 'part of the package' which their employers owe them. In 1993, 16 000 Cape Town municipal workers took 108317 days 'sick leave' in just 6 months. That is the equivalent of 297 years of time-off, paid for by the rate-payers. That's over 13 sick-leave days per person p.a. Parents write excuse notes saying their child is ill, when they actually want a few extra days' holiday to suit the family. (What does this teach the child about lying?) (Reader's Digest July 1994)

Sick leave costs South Africa millions. Some employees believe that sick-leave days are a "benefit" to which they are entitled, like annual leave. (Sunday Times 14.8.2005).

Thornville Sawmill manager John Houtson hit the roof when he saw a newspaper photograph of employee Nick Hebron entertaining crowds at the Royal Show. He had called in sick with a doctor's note at 8am on Monday. There he was, grinning into the camera with a Brazilian iguana on his shoulder. Houtson said that Hebron had worked for him for 2 years, but was already one year in arrears for sick leave. He refuses to pay an employee, who should have been recuperating at home, enjoying himself at the Royal Show. So, the headline wryly comments, "If you take sick leave don't get photographed." Faking sick leave is a perennial problem that costs employers millions of rands.

**How Do You Feel About These Examples? Admiration? Or Disgust**

***

# Capsule 3 An Example of Medical Fraud from Germany

If Medical Corruption is possible in super-efficient Germany, how much more likely that it could happen in less regulated countries? The German Medical Association has investigated nearly 1,000 cases of corrupt doctors over the past few years, according to its president, Frank Ulrich Montgomery.

Dr Montgomery told Der Spiegel that more than half of the case involved alleged bribes from an Israeli pharmaceutical company, Ratiopharm. The doctors were paid for prescribing its drugs to their patients. This was "clearly prohibited", says Dr Montgomery.

"The Medical Association punished 163 Ratiopharm doctors after state prosecutors made the files available to us. ... This ongoing corruption debate is a thorn in our flesh which is massively damaging the reputation of my profession," Montgomery told Der Spiegel.

The problem is most acute for transplant surgeons. Two senior doctors in Leipzig have been suspended after an investigation showed that they had manipulated records to push 38 liver patients up the waiting list for organs. Similar cases have been reported in Göttingen, Munich and Regensburg. **http://www.bioedge.org/index.php/bioethics/ bioethics_article/10362.**

The government and the Medical Association have reassured the public that corruption in the transplant waiting list has been eradicated. But the media seems convinced that public confidence in the integrity of the transplant system has been shaken.

The *Frankfurter Allgemeine Zeitung* writes: "The damage done is immense. That is obviously not just true of patients on the waiting list for donated organs who were cheated. That is also true of all patients who see themselves as being literally helpless. And it is true of donors, whose mistrust grows with each case of manipulation. The number of donor organs began dropping last year just as the first cases of deceit became public. Last but not least, such cases also hurt transplant doctors, whose own area of specialization has been plunged into disrepute. And the disappearance of trust in how livers, hearts and kidneys are handled hurts the standing of all doctors. As such, it is all the more in their interest to combat this growing damage to their image."

**Would You Be An Organ Donor In Such Circumstances?**

Yes _____ Maybe _____ Unlikely _____ No _____

***

# Capsule 4 Medical Aid, Insurance, Selling Jobs, Conniving Contracts

## Medical Aid Scams

I saw a queue forming outside a doctor's surgery. My colleague explained that the 'patients had financial ailments rather than medical ones, and the doctor was treating the symptoms with other people's money'. The system involved a prescription that was never filled. The doctor paid the now-healed patient 80% of the value of the medicines in cash, pocketing the balance when the medical aid payment arrived. Everyone was happy except the honest idiots whose medical aid premiums went up more steeply than a space shuttle on lift-off. (Doug Morton in the Witness 5.8.99)

A reporter asked the doctor's receptionist upfront whether it was possible to get a prescription to purchase "groceries" from the pharmacy. "There's no problem as long as you have a medical aid" she answered. In the doctor's room the reporter told the doctor she wanted a prescription to buy "groceries". "Hmm, what shall we say you are suffering from? You have a bladder infection." the doctor said, writing out a script for Ciprobay, Citrocit and Buscopan. The reporter went to a Woodlands pharmacy, explained she wanted "groceries", and was given a voucher for R151. The assistant phoned the Medical Aid to confirm the reporter was a member. The reporter then bought deodorant, toothpaste, baby food and dishwashing liquid, worth R84. The difference was carried forward as a credit. No receipt or till-slip was issued when requested. A similar scam operated at a Church Street pharmacy. A young woman in the queue told her that many in the crowd had come to stock up on groceries - "the pharmacy has been helping me for quite some time now. I buy mainly expensive perfume, and also bought expensive sunglasses." (Witness 2 August 1999). As a result of exposing this scam, Medscheme director Gary Tailor reported that three doctors have been caught and they had recovered about R1 million. Nationally, Medscheme had recovered over R11.3 million. "Medical Aid fraud exists because patients participate in the crime. We urge patients not to turn a blind eye to fraud and corruption" (Witness 13.12.99)

### Insurance fraud

Angelo Haggiyannes, when Witwatersrand's Regional Director of Auto & General, reported that "Insurance companies are forced by mounting claims to raise their premiums by between 15 and 30 percent in 1993. A main reason is fraudulent claims. The honest client must foot the bill for the minority who see a claim not as compensation for a loss, but as an opportunity to enrich themselves."

### Cash for Jobs Scam

Busisiwe Manyoni was arrested in 2002 for selling non-existent jobs to desperately poor people. While out on bail she went to Mpumalanga and scammed the poor there. She was eventually given a suspended sentence under correctional supervision, and now she has been re-arrested for the same crime: selling non-existent jobs. (Witness 20.7.2004)

### Civil Servants get Contracts with Government

In just 2 years (ending March 2007) 916 Civil servants and their spouses benefited from R136 million worth of government tenders in KwaZulu-Natal. Most of these were from the Departments of Education and Health. Examples included: Health department's employee

P Rajaruthnam's Isipingo Hospital business earned R5 418 545 for doing business with his department. D.V. Zondo of Sokotshane Forestry and Construction, who works in the Dept of Agriculture and Environmental Affairs, did work for government totaling R8 3465 973. (Many others are listed). Members of the Legislature called for the naming and shaming of public servants who moonlight as business owners contracted to their employers. (Weekend Witness 24.10.2009).

Three years later the Auditor General named 'municipal staff doing business with their employer' as a "key area of concern". (Witness 26.1.2012)

**How Do You Feel About These Examples? Admiration? ___Disgust?___**

# Capsule 5 Tenderpreneurs

This is the new job Description for those who obtain lucrative government tenders without following standard regulations. They get the advantages of Government favours through the back door.

Wikipedia explains: "Tenderpreneur" is a South African government official or politician who uses their powers and influence to secure government tenders and contracts. The word is a portmanteau of "tendering" and "entrepreneur." The Star, a South African newspaper, describes a tenderpreneur as "someone politically well-connected who has got rich through the government tendering system". In January 2010, South African Communist Party leader Blade Nzimande called for transparency in the awarding of tenders, saying "let's be bold, let's go and promote small entrepreneurs, and defeat tenderpreneurs, those who steal."

Terry Mackenzie-hoy (Martin Creamer Engineering News) gives personal experience of how Tenderpreneurship works in practice: Let us take two relatively recent occurrences: "About ten years ago, we were in a joint venture to bid on the supply of audio equipment (microphones, amplifiers, recording equipment, design services, and so on) to Parliament.

The tender rules were that we had to employ a professional engineer, we had to have fully owned black economic-empowerment partner and we had to be associated with an international firm which had done similar work. We ticked all these boxes. We had to submit five copies of our tender to the Parliamentary office in Cape Town at a certain time. We (and others) did this. At opening time, one of the Parliamentary staff took all the tenders out of the box and started walking off. "Hey," we said, "read out the tenders!" So he did. When this was done, he said: "I have another tender, in a safe. I haven't got the key." We started arguing with him. He went off with his cellphone and called somebody. Back he came and said: "Wait." So we did. After

20 minutes, a man sprinted into the room with a tender document. The two disappeared to another office and then came back and read out the price of the newly arrived tender. Guess what? It was the lowest.

Further, in 2008 a number of tenderers (26 in all) bid on supplying consultancy services to supervise the construction of public toilets for a municipality. Among them was a well known consultancy. It was stated that the successful tender would be the one which had the highest points, based on a set number of criteria.

The consultancy got the most points and the bid evaluation committee recommended that it be appointed. Then the municipality wrote back and said they were going to amend the criteria for award, which they did. The consultancy was still the highest. No award resulted and the consultancy was then told that the tender would be re-advertised.

So it went to court while the tender was split between four firms. The judge found that the consultancy should have sought an interdict earlier on in the matter and dismissed the appeal with costs. The simple lesson is this – no amount of rearrangement of tender style will change things if the people giving out the work have no shame at all in how they manipulate the tenders. And they clearly do not. In the consultancy's case, the bid evaluation committee recommended its appointment but was turned aside. What could the consultancy do but go to court? It is not the system that is wrong – it is the people who shamelessly abuse it, and that's really wrong."
**http://www.engineeringnews.co.za/article/tenderpreneurs-part-ii-2013-02-15**

Prior to the Football World Cup in South Africa (2010) tenders were invited to construct stadia. Some of the largest civil engineering construction firms connived to wangle the contracts at inflated prices, paid for by the tax-payers. This was tenderpreneurship on a massive scale. Such scandal-news breaks with regular monotony in the media. The richest barons are greedy for the huge profits that can be turned on a lucrative Government tender.

**How do you feel about these examples? Admiration? ___ Disgust? ___**

***

# Capsule 6 When Bribery Is The Norm

A missionary from South Africa tells this story...

"There may have been a time in your life where you feel that you have no choice but to sin and disobey God. Perhaps you feel like there is no way out, but there is. It often doesn't look like a way out or we don't understand it, but God does not put you in situations to tempt you into sinning. That would be going against His Holy character, it would be going against His very nature.

There was a situation when I helped run the coffee shop in China. In China bribery is seen as the norm. If you want to get something done, you need to give the right person an expensive gift or something like that. In the coffee shop there were these official government receipts for tax purposes. When the receipts had run out, you take the book back to the government department and they would renew them for you. When the receipts ran out one day, we wanted to take the books back to get new ones, but we couldn't find the books. They *simply* had gone missing. So we went to the accountant who deals with these kinds of things and she said that this is going to cause a lot of problems and is going to be a mission to sort out so we will have to offer a 'admin fee' of 1000 yuan or else will have to pay a fine of 10 000 yuan.

We decided that we are going to do the right thing and pay the 10 000 even though the shop was struggling financially and was in the red. So we prayed that the Lord would handle the situation and when one of the staff went to the government department to apply for new receipt books, she managed to sort it all out legally and only pay 500 for the new books. That was such a testimony to the staff because even though they were believers they couldn't understand why you would pay 10 000 when you could pay 1000. The Lord really showed us that day that even though you are in a tough position and there seems like no way out, being obedient is always the right thing." (Reproduced by permission)

*Author's comment......* This remarkable outcome of paying only 500 yuan instead of a 1000 yuan bribe cannot be guaranteed in all circumstances! People of Integrity must be prepared to pay the cost of Integrity in fighting the temptation to fraud and corruption.

# Part Two

# Fight Corruption with Integrity

# Capsule 7 Standing Against By Standing For

Yes, we want to fight against this Fraud and Corruption

> that is sabotaging good governance and eroding the viability of business, that is ruining our Nation, and oppressing the poor and powerless.

But the best way to fight evil is to champion what is good.

We begin by shaking ourselves into a Positive Mind-set.

Yes it's good to stand up and protest against Fraud and Corruption.

Competing Political Parties find common ground when they Fight Corruption.

But let's go beyond Protest, beyond "Fighting AGAINST", beyond a negative goal ....

Let's fight FOR something Positive. Let's embrace a positive goal:


## INTEGRITY

When we stand FOR Integrity

> we will automatically be standing AGAINST Fraud and Corruption.
> Integrity gives one moral credibility in fighting Fraud and Corruption.

But can one stand AGAINST Fraud and Corruption, without standing FOR Integrity? The fight against Fraud and Corruption is undermined and discredited if the fighters themselves do not have personal Integrity.

If each of us can become a person of INTEGRITY, then we will instill an internal firewall that will protect us from Fraud and Corruption. We will strengthen our moral immune system to resist Fraud and Corruption.

With Integrity woven into our characters, we will have a strong defense against Temptation.

**So, what is this strong characteristic called "Integrity"? How do we identify it, explain it?**

\*\*\*

# Capsule 8 Defining Integrity

**"Being an integrated person of virtue in whom are no hidden contradictions"**

*"Being"* is deeper than 'knowing' or 'doing'.

It is the essence of who I am. It is part of my identity.

*"An Integrated Person"* ~
every part of me is connected, in harmony: Body, Mind and Spirit

My Physical, Emotional, Mental, Religious, Social aspects live coherently as one.

No civil war rages within me.

I am at peace with myself, towards others and with God.

*"Of Virtue"* ~ Because some people are 'integrated' in *Evil*,

it is necessary to emphasise that a person of Integrity, who stands against Fraud and Corruption

is a person of *Virtue* - regarded by others as basically good. (This does not mean that they are morally Perfect. No-one is perfect!)

"Integrity" is associated with a positive, wholesome character.

*"No Hidden Contradictions"* ~ Not saying one thing and doing another.

The opposite of "Integrity" is "Hypocrisy".

One's Private and Public lives are run by the same rules.
You are who you are when no-one is looking.

## PUBLIC AND PRIVATE

You have heard people say:

*"It doesn't matter what a person does in private, as long as they do a good job in public"*

This is true in certain skills:
A rapist can be a good accountant
A thief can be a good musician

A liar can be a good carpenter

So, would you employ such a person as your accountant, musician or carpenter? Probably not ... Why? ...

because you cannot TRUST them.

They lack INTEGRITY.


If you cannot trust someone in Private,
    how can you trust them in Public?
    If she breaks her marriage vows,
    what stops her from breaking her business promises?
    INTEGRITY embraces the whole of life: PUBLIC **and** PRIVATE.
    It includes these Virtues:

Honesty, Truthfulness, Faithfulness, Trustworthiness, Dependability, Accountability, Transparency, Self-discipline, Consistency, Loyalty.

Would you like your 'Letter of Commendation' for your next job to list the above qualities?

Or ~ would you want a reputation for being ...

Dishonest, a Liar, Unfaithful, Deceitful, Unreliable, Devious, Sly, Unaccountable, Undisciplined, Inconsistent, Disloyal?

INTEGRITY BUILDS TRUST ~
How long does it take to build Trust? ..........
HYPOCRISY DESTROYS TRUST~
How long does it take to destroy Trust? ..........
*INTEGRITY is the prize we aim for, in our better moments!*

***

# Capsule 9 Integrity Builds a Strong Immune System

## That Will Resist The Temptation To Fraud And Corruption

*Fraud* and *Corruption* are deadly viruses,

which threaten the economic and moral health of the nation. Ultimately the very survival of the State is at risk.

Every individual in the nation can contract these viruses. They attack through insidious and effective Temptations.

### DEFINING FRAUD

"A deliberate misrepresentation or perversion of the truth which results in prejudice,

actual or potential, to another person." (Family Guide to Law in South Africa, Reader's Digest 1984)

"An intentional untruth or a dishonest scheme used to take unfair advantage of another

person, or group of persons." (World Book 1976 Vol 7 Article 'Fraud')

### DEFINING CORRUPTION

"Individuals using their position to use corporate resources for personal gain" (Delegates from 43 African nations at a Corruption Summit in Addis Ababa 19.2.2002)

"The giving of a benefit is corrupt when it is done with the intention of influencing the recipient of the benefit to perform or disregard his duty, so as to give the donor of the benefit an unfair advantage over others, or as a reward for having done so before the benefit is given" (Judge Hilary Squires, reported Sunday Times 5.6.2006)

This book uses the terms "Fraud" and "Corruption" either together or interchangeably. They include Dishonesty, Lies, Theft, Cadre-deployment and Nepotism, usually for personal gain at the expense of others, or of the general public.

**Note:** Fraud and Corruption occur in all sectors:

Government at all levels,
Businesses of all sizes,
Religious contexts of all faiths
Non-government organisations (NGOs)
Non-profit organisations (NPOs)
Community-based organisations (CBOs)
Faith-based organisations (FBOs)

*The world loses over US$1trillion through corruption every year.*
*Africa loses 25% of its gross wealth by Corruption (US$150b / yr)*
**#EXPOSED2013**
Fraud and Corruption are usually committed by the middle- and upper-classes. The 'benefits' of Fraud and Corruption are usually financial and material, but can also be favours, fame, prestige, sex or power.

Corruption is a Spiritual problem.

"The precedence of material needs over the spiritual

is the basic factor that has encouraged corruption. Material values have become the criterion of success."

(South African President Thabo Mbeki, opening the International Conference on Corruption 10.10.1999)

If someone tells you that so-and-so is "doing well for herself",

do you think of someone living like Mother Theresa?

Probably 'No'.

Do you think of someone living in affluent material wealth? Probably 'Yes'.

That's a graphic indicator of how Materialism has defined our thinking.

# Part Three

# Pre-conditions for Corruption

# Capsule 10 Essential Pre-Conditions for Fraud and

# Corruption: Opportunity - The External Factor (The Outside Story) Greed - The Internal Factor (The Inside Story)

If either are missing, Fraud and Corruption are unlikely to occur. If both are present, the Temptation grows stronger. The likelihood of Fraud and Corruption is greater.

How do you deal with the External Factor - "Opportunity"?

By: Audits, Accountability Structures, Corruption Watch, Policing, the Courts of Justice.

How do you deal with the Internal Factor - "Greed"?

You hold in your hands these *Immunity-booster Capsules* which help to defend you from it. But before continuing with this immunising course, we must examine the *External Factor of Opportunity...*

How to recognise and deal with Opportunity for Fraud and Corruption is "The Outside Story". This is the story we read in the papers. This is the subject of debates in Parliament. Our Courts deal with the Outside Story of Fraud and Corruption. Many Government Departments and Para-State Entities have "Corruption Hotlines". Many Business Enterprises have numbers you can phone, even anonymously, to report Fraud. On the 31st January 2012 Cosatu and others launched **"Corruption Watch"**, and have achieved modest success as people have reported to .....

http://www.corruptionwatch.org.za/content/
make-your-complaint

Have you been a victim of corruption? Are you aware of corrupt activity? Open this web-site and click on the red *Report an Incident using the button* on the right. They also list official bodies and NGOs that may be able to help you if you know of, any corrupt activity.

EXPOSED2013 was an international Programme to mobilise 100 million people in 100 countries to take action against Corruption, climaxing in an Event 14-20 October 2013. It had the backing of major international NGOs. Check out their website:
**http://www.exposed2013.com**

**Unashamedly Ethical** is South African based, with an international footprint, working for ethical relationships (interpersonal and corporate) and for clean living. It is part of the battle for integrity against Fraud and Corruption. More of this later, as U.E operates in both the External and Internal domains, in the fight against Fraud and Corruption. It welcomes signatories to its Pledge, and holds all signatories accountable through an Ombudsman. Read more, and sign the Pledge at **http://www.unashamedlyethical.com**

For a Directory of strategic contact details **https://www.gov.za/ about-government/contact-directory/national-government**

For a Discussion on Whistle-blowing: See Capsule 41
**Have You Checked Out Any Of These Web-Sites?**
**Yes/No /I plan to**

# Part Four

# Corruption-the OUTSIDE story:
# Opportunity

# Capsule 11 Public Opportunity Is Fuelled By...

- Inadequate monitoring, audits and accountability structures

- Copying methods used by others to fiddle the system
- Whistle-blowers are not taken seriously, ignored or even punished. Example: Muller exposed 130 false licences a day issued fraudulently by a Mpumalanga Traffic Office. He lost his job, no other traffic department would employ him, and he was dependent on his wife's income till he died, a dejected man, in 2005.

- The boss himself is corrupt. "If she fingers me, I'll finger her. We're already in it together"

*If either "Personal Greed" or "Public Opportunity" is missing, the Temptation falls away. For Temptation to occur, there must be both the internal greed and the external opportunity.*

*The onus is on each person to deal with the Greed of his/her heart.* The antidote for GREED is Contentment

*"Godliness with Contentment is great gain. Those who want to get rich fall into temptation" (Bible 2 Timothy 6:6,9)*

**Consult Unashamedly Ethical
for help in developing an anti-corruption Ethic.**

https://www.unashamedlyethical.com

Info@unashamedlyethical.com

*The onus is on the State, the Firm/Corporate/Employer, the Department/NGO/Religion to ensure that Opportunity is absent.* The antidote for OPPORTUNITY is Audit Accountability.

An external authority with a reputation for impartial Integrity must audit policies, procedures, decisions, and finances.

*People do what you INspect, not what you EXpect!*

**Consult Corruption Watch and/or Accountability Now for help in building structural deterrents to Corruption**

https://www.corruptionwatch.org.za
report@corruptionwatch.org.za


https://accountabilitynow.org.za

# Part Five

# Corruption-the INSIDE story: GREED

# Capsule 12 Fraud and Corruption ~ the Inside Story

While much effort goes into dealing with the External Opportunity factor in temptation, little investment is made in combating the Internal Greed factor.

Greed is a vicious virus, very difficult to recognise, and even more difficult to overcome.

We are reluctant to wage war against Greed, because (let's face it) we enjoy it.

So, while doing all we can to deal with "The Outside Story of Corruption", Opportunity, we must also work hard at dealing with "The Inside Story of Corruption", Greed.

***That's why this book is titled "Fraud and Corruption ~ the Inside Story"***
It enters relatively unexplored territory, inside the human heart:

How do you recognise Greed?

What fuels Greed?
How do you recognise the Temptation to Greed?
What is the weak point in your defenses against Greed?
How can you downsize Greed?
What is the antidote to Greed?

Let's begin this journey into the Interior, and see what we can learn.
It's time to admit that Greed lives inside every person, to a greater or lesser extent.

Greed is part of the human condition.
Greed lurks inside *ME*.

Yes, get angry with Fraud and Corruption committed by other people.

That's OK. That's right.
But first get angry with the seeds of Greed in your own heart.
Seeds waiting to germinate into the sins of Fraud and Corruption.

It's easy to see Greed in other people.

It's more difficult to detect it in yourself.

*"Why do you try to take the speck out of your brother's eye, when you have a log in your own?*

*First take the log out of your own eye,*

*then you will see clearly to take the speck out of your brother's eye."* Jesus, in the Gospel of Matthew 7:3-5

While most Strategies to fight Dishonesty have targeted Policing to remove Opportunity, this Book aims to strengthen your Immunity to the Internal Factor of GREED.

**GREED ~ THE SOURCE OF TEMPTATION TO FRAUD AND CORRUPTION**

On a scale of 0 (No Greed whatsoever) to 10 (Driven by Greed) ~
**How Greedy Are You?** _____

# Capsule 13 It's All In The Mind

This 2000 year old quotation puts its finger on the source of Corruption:

*"Your way of life is corrupt through deceitful desires, so be renewed in your minds"* (St Paul, Ephesians 4:22,23).

Greed causes us to be corrupt.

Greed is a desire.
Greed is a desire of the mind.
Greed affects the way we live.

Greed is a deceitful desire, deceiving us to think it is right...
"I deserve what I desire".
So we must deal with Greed at its source: in our minds.
It's all in the Mind.

We need *"to be renewed in our minds"*.
We need new minds.

How can we get this new un-greedy mind?

*"Let each of you look not only to his own interests, but also to the interests of others. Have this mind in you, which is yours in Christ Jesus"* (St Paul, Philippians 2:4,5)

Don't be selfish, thinking only of your own interests. Think of others .... those who have less than you do,

the poor who are robbed by fraud and corruption.

"Ordinary people bear the cost of corruption.

It is the poor, particularly women, who suffer the greatest burden. The payment of a bribe can mean hunger for a whole family."

(Transparency International Global Corruption Barometer 2013)


Look out for the interests of Others! Don't be so self-centred that you become Greedy.

That opens the door to Fraud, Theft and Corruption.

The supreme example of un-greedy selfless caring for the interests of Others is Jesus Christ. He was *"equal with God"*,

but he let go of the privileges this highest rank entitled him to.

Instead, he *"made himself nothing, became a servant, and was born"* as a baby in Bethlehem. *As a human being, he humbled himself,*

*and eventually died on a cross.* (Philippians 2:6-8)
No-one has ever taken a greater Demotion than Jesus Christ.

He voluntarily made this enormous self-sacrifice
for the benefit of us self-centred, greedy, corrupt sinners.

*"He showed his love for us in that, while we were still sinners, Christ died for us."* (Rom ans 5:8)
That's the Mind we should have - *"the mind that was in Christ Jesus".*

When the unselfish Mind of Jesus

replaces the selfish Mind of Greed which we've inherited, then we will not have those deceitful greedy desires

which predispose us to fraud, theft and corruption.

On a scale of 0 (No Selfishness whatsoever) to 10 (Driven by Selfishness)

**How Selfish Are You?** _____

\*\*\*

# Capsule 14 How Do I Recognise Greed?

What is the difference between **GREED** and **NEED**?

*(Note: The figures given in the following examples are relative, increasing monthly with inflation.)*

Some people will say they need R50 000 per month to cover their expenses.

Others can manage to live on, say, R5 000 per month.

Both justify what they demand by listing their requirements and adding them up.

Some will say they 'need' a new car, costing R500 000.

Others will be happy to own a second-hand car worth R50 000

Others view any car to be as unattainable as a Boeing airplane. They go by taxi.

Some will insist on sending their children to a private school, costing R10 000 per month.

Others will consider themselves to be lucky to get a place in a former Model C school.

Others will be grateful for the No-fee Government school.
Trade Unions mobilise strike action for "decent jobs" and "a living wage".

How do we describe a "decent" job?

How do we quantify, in money-terms, a "living" wage?

Those gaunt men who stand alongside the street waiting for job offers will take *any* job.

Most will be grateful for a once-off day-job, or some piece-work.

Many will envy those who have the most menial jobs ~ better than no job at all.

Those farm-workers who went on the rampage protesting their low minimum wage had been "living" on the low wage they had been paid, and now, fuelled by anger,

they had the strength to move rocks onto the highway, and demolish property.

Whenever one tries to quantify this "living wage", the figures can be disputed.

One person will be able to "live" on a low wage and still save something each month.

Another cannot "live" on that same wage,

going deeper into debt each month.

How long is a piece of string?

Living Wage Individual in South Africa is expected to reach R6700 per month by the end of 2020, according to Trading Economics global macro models and analysts expectations. In the long-term, the South Africa Living Wage Individual is projected to trend around R6700 per month in 2021, according to our econometric models.

**https://www.bing.com/
search?q=what+is+Living+Wage+in+South+Africa+2020**

What is life like at the upper end?

> (That's where most of the fraud and corruption is happening.)

> The average salary for those living in the more affluent cities is R300 000 per annum(R25000 per month) The cost of living varies between R75 000 and R27 000

> The city-by-city difference between Cost-of-Living and Salary is reflected in this website:
> **https://www.myjobmag.co.za/blog/cost-of-living-vs-salary-in-south-africa**

*What does this tell us about "Greed" and "Need"?*

**Who** **are** **the** Needy
**Ones?**_____

**Who** **are** **the** Greedy **Ones?**
_____

\*\*\*

# Capsule 15 Upmarket Greed

In 2003, Moferefere Lekorotsoana, of the National Union of Mineworkers, described as "obscene" the fact that Non-Executive Mine Directors get 1400 x the salary of miners who do the actual work in the mines.

Was it always like this? Consider this 40-year comparison (in South Africa):

> 1973: CEO was paid 25 x the salary of the average worker
> 2003: CEO the pay was 600 x the salary of the average worker
> 2013: Top 60 Executives earn 1700 x average worker wage.
> (Safm News 18.12.2013)

The Wage Gap has widened enormously in recent years.
*(Labour Research Services survey July 2005)*

> The worker-to-executive remuneration gap ratio grew from 1-to-46 to 1-to-92. It almost doubled.

The Guardian newspaper (in the United Kingdom) shed 100 staff to help stem losses. The staff argued they should "Cap the bosses salaries at £100 000 per annum (R1 600 000)".
But the CEO [at £576 000pa (R9 216 000)] didn't agree"

(Church Chronicles May 2013)

'Percentage' increases in salaries actually worsen the Gap:

> In 2005 a "percentage increase" across the board raised the lowest paid by R25 pm

and the highest paid by many thousands of rands per month. The gap grows.

This led to a series of strikes in SA Airways, Municipalities and Mining.

Within a few years of Democracy in South Africa, some Directors were paid R1.6 million per annum simply to sit on a Board. Some individuals are on many Boards, creaming the money.

Black Economic Empowerment laws mean that the demand for skilled, qualified Directors exceeds the supply.

Head-hunters poach by offering ever higher packages, and this exacerbates the problem.

This also fuels an exaggerated sense of self-worth and a greed for "obscene" salaries and perks.
### This is a worldwide phenomenon:

"The Pay for chief executives is ludicrously high"
(*Academy of Management in United States*)

### Relative Wealth
How do South African Executives compare with those in other countries?

"There is little doubt that South African executives are generously remunerated by global standards. *P E Corporate Services* conducts an annual survey of remuneration earned by executives, and resultant net disposable income, in a number of developed and developing countries around the world. Net disposable income is defined in this context as the net income available to an executive after deducting tax and social security costs as well as essential living costs (food, housing, travel, utilities, education, etc.) from gross income. The buying power of this net disposable income is then measured by a net wealth index which compares relative buying power within each country included in the study. South African executives enjoyed a number one world ranking in this study between 2009 and 2011, topping the U.S.A. - the traditional leaders in net wealth for most of the 34 years that this study has been carried out.

The 2012 study ranked South African executives second (at 100), marginally behind the U.S.A. (at 104), as can be seen from the list below."

**http://www.pecs.co.za/index.php/the-wage-gap-south-africa-s-emotive-issue**

| | | | |
|---|---|---|---|
| U. S. A.   104 15% | U. K. | 78 14% Namibia   69 56% | Belgium 49 |
| South Africa 100 50% | Zambia | 75 64% Zimbabwe 55 68% | Malawi          4 |
| Germany 89   16% | Australia | 74 n/a  Nigeria     50 70% | |
| Kenya    84   50% | Botswana 72 | 30% France     47 n/a | |

% = Percentage of those living below the Poverty Line ~ vividly illustrating the Wage Gaps. Source: **http://www.indexmundi.com/g/r.aspx?v=69**

This shows the INEQUALITY which our government aims to remove from our nation. We should reduce the "100" - the obscene wealth of the many super-rich, and reduce the "50%" of our citizens living in abject poverty. Confront the demon of Inequality from BOTH ends.

*Especially because it is those who are already-rich, the more highly paid, whose Greed for More leads to Corruption!*

*Get Angry! Get Angrier!*

***

# Capsule 16 Bribing Officials to Have Integrity

A bizarre story unfolded in July 2013. President Zuma announced that the Auditor-General would receive a pay-rise of nearly R941 400 pa. His salary would increase from R1 708 600 pa to R2 650 000. Over R220 000 per month. This, he said, would put it on par with the salary of a Judge.

Backdated seven years to 2006, Mr Nombembe would also receive a lump sum windfall of R6 589 800!

Listen to the imaginary thoughts of middle-class civil servants: "Nombembe's present salary of R1 708 600 pa is over the top - I come out on my salary of R240 000" says one. "I'm able to survive on R180 000 pa" says another. "But this man gets 7 to 9 times as much."

What was more bizarre was the general approval of others for this astronomical rise in salary. The General Secretary of the largest Trade Union federation in South Africa, Mr Zwelinzima Vavi, also approved. He now has precedence-setting leverage to get huge pay-rises for all the workers in the country. But will he succeed? Where will the money come from?

Even more bizarre was the approval of the official Opposition Their MP argued that **this enormous salary was necessary to prevent the Auditor-General from yielding to Corruption. Effectively he was proclaiming that the Auditor-General needed a huge Bribe to prevent him from being Corrupt!** Without this colossal gift, we would not be able to trust the Auditor-General to have Integrity. This is a shocking insight into the depth of moral decadence into which South Africa's attitude to Corruption has tumbled. It assumes that we can't trust anyone to stay clean, so we must officially grease their palms with 6-figure bribes so that those same palms will not be unofficially greased by others.

Now everyone can climb onto the band-wagon. "Boss, I need a huge rise, otherwise I'm afraid I'll have to take bribes to satisfy my greed for opulence." Shame on the Government (ANC) and the Opposition (DA) for collaborating in such expensive Corruption. You have set in motion a process that panders to Greed. After all, what does a man do with so much money? He already gets more than the average man would ever dream of getting (I use the word 'get', not 'earned'. No 'work' anyone does can be worth such obscene 'earnings'.)

See the Hypocrisy of President Zuma's beneficence: His official ANC Manifesto is *"to fight the triple scourge of Poverty, Inequality and Unemployment"*. Yet in this one decision he makes the Rich richer, the Inequality ratio wider and he condemns more people to Unemployment and Poverty. How many new jobs could have been created with Mr Nombembe's windfall? He also adds fuel to the Labour Union's demands fomenting unrest in the country.

By paying such an over-the-top salary, our President, and those who endorse it, are telling every employee: "If you don't get these huge salary increases, you are entitled to improve your personal income by any means you like - by theft, fraud or corruption." With that message on the billboards of South Africa, we may as well give up on the fight against Fraud and Corruption right now. It's a lost cause. The newly prized Values of Fraud and Corruption will replace the out-of-date Values of Integrity, Accountability and honest Work. The unspoken assumption is that a person must be paid extra so that s/he will be honest. Otherwise s/he will steal from the public purse.

This MUST not happen!

Commit yourself to a life of Integrity, and spurn all signals that tempt you into wrong-doing.

*On the next page is a Questionnaire that will help you*
*rate your own vulnerability to the Temptation to Corruption.*
*If it will help you answer honestly, keep your replies confidential.*

# Keep a record of your answers so that you can compare them later.

## Capsule 17 Which Temptations Are Likely To Conquer You?

*Go through this Checklist.... Know your Weak Points.... Fortify yourself to resist*

*Rate your Vulnerability:*

**5 = Irresistible Temptation; 4 = Strong Temptation; 3 = Modest Temptation 2 = Weak Temptation; 1 = Very Weak Temptation; 0 = No Temptation at all**

**SEE CAPSULE:**

1 - Nobody will know if I commit fraud

1 - The opportunity is there, so why not take it?

18 - I don't want to let my Family down

18 - I want to give my kids the best start in life - they must have what others have

19 - I am trying to keep up with the Joneses

20 - I want to live the best life

21 - My worth is measured by my wealth

21 - The affluent life-style boosts my self-esteem

21 - I feel I've achieved in life if I am wealthy or .... I have accumulated assets

22 - I suffered before/under apartheid, so now it's my time to get rich

23 - I am worth more than I am being paid

24 - Others get paid more than I am paid

25 - I am being treated unjustly

26 - If I had more money I'd have more power

26 - I can use my power to get more money

Other people are doing fraud and/or corruption, so why can't I?

My boss is doing fraud and/or corruption, so if he fingers me I can finger him

Other people got away with it, so I can too

It's just a small amount

In this world, we cannot avoid Temptation. It lurks behind many of life's circumstances.

> It is wise to imagine, *before* you are tempted, how you would handle the temptation.

> Being prepared ahead of time will help you resist it when temptation strikes.

**Commit yourself NOW to live a life of INTEGRITY,**

**and resist the Temptations to compromise your INTEGRITY.**

**Temptations will assault each of us in different ways:**
**BE PREPARED!**

# Part Six

# Excuses for Greed

# Capsule 18 Excuses For Greed: "I Don't Want To Let My Family Down"

*"I don't want to let my family down"*
A true story....
This father wanted to give his wife and children the best of everything.

Soon they were living in a posh home with all the mod-cons.

Two upmarket cars and a speed-boat on a trailer occupied their three garages.

The children enjoyed top-rate education at the best private schools.

Of course he had a good job: he was senior Financial Manager for a large corporation.

He could afford his lifestyle.
Except that he couldn't.
But his job gave him the *Opportunity* for Fraud. He managed it easily.

When his bubble burst, as bubbles do, he lost his job

and was sentenced to 2 years free board and lodging at our expense.
On his release, he received financial and lifestyle counselling.

Moving to Gauteng, he was employed by another large corporation as .... you guessed it:

Financial Manager.

He wanted to make up to his family for the distress he had caused them.

And the only way he knew how was to spoil them with material luxuries.

This time he was sentenced to 10 years in prison. *(So - did he let his family down?)*

### "I want to give my kids the best start in life - they must have what others have"

How do you define "best"? Does it mean "having everything they want"?

Then you a training your kids to be Greedy for 'stuff'.
Then they are likely to indulge in fraud and corruption.
Don't be surprised when they do crime when they grow up.
Crime is more lucrative than honest salaried work.

If your kids get everything they want, free, without earning it, they'll expect this when older.

But real life is not like that. There are no "free lunches". Unless you steal them. *Is teaching your kids that everything in life is free 'the best start' for them?*

This breeds the Culture of Entitlement which is eroding the moral fibre of the nation.

To get votes, politicians make generous promises: Free houses, water, electricity etc.

But no Government has the resources to provide these without Tax-income.

The People believe they are entitled to get all the promised freebies.

They vent their frustration through riots that vandalise,

destroying schools, clinics, buses, trains, infrastructure.

*Is breeding such a Culture of Entitlement "the best start" you can give your kids? ......*

If your kids complain that others have what they haven't, and you yield to their manipulation, you are teaching them that "Others, more affluent than your family, set life's standards"

*Do you want to train your kids to "Keep up with the Joneses'?* [See Capsule 19]

**To give your kids the best start in life ...**

Teach them, by example, by word and by practical training, to choose strong Values.

Economic Values: e.g. Hard Work, a Good Work Ethic, Learning & Earning, Honesty.

Moral Values: e.g. Integrity, Compassion for Others, Kindness, Sexual Purity.

Teach them that "you reap what you sow". No sowing, no (honest) reaping.

The Law of Consequences always works ... in the end, it cannot be avoided.

A strong Value-system will be a lasting Foundation for life, beyond what Materialism can offer.

Children from poorer families usually have stronger characters than affluent children.

***

# Capsule 19 More Excuses For Greed: "Keep Up With the Joneses"

*"I want to keep up with the Joneses"*
We all know the power of this temptation.

We all compare ourselves with others who have more than we do ~ "The Joneses". (We never compare ourselves with those who have less)

Driven by Envy and Jealousy (though we'd never admit it), we watch them and copy them and covet what they've got.

Then we aspire to BE "the Joneses", and this makes *others* envious.

Even if we must dive into debt to make it happen.

1. Who are "the Joneses" in your life, the people you want to compete with? Name them.

1. Are they important to you because of **what** they have? Or because of **who** they are?

1. Is their Value in their "stuff"? Or is their Value in their characters?

1. Are their life-Values worth emulating? Are they worth envying?

Strip their material assets away from them:

their upmarket home, latest gadgets, luxury cars,

their overseas holidays, fashion clothing, professional status in society ....

What is left to envy?

Don't be mesmerised by their Material Success. It can disappear in a moment.

Ask the Nebuchadnezzars, the Malemas and the J Arthur Browns of this world.
(Also, many of the envied 'Joneses' have more Debt than we'd wish to have.)

Long ago one of the most respected moral leaders of his day sat down to evaluate his life.

Using the Ten Commandments as his check-list, he ticked every one.

Yes. Yes. Yes. Yes. Yes. Yes. Yes. Yes. Yes. ........ No.

The tenth one stabbed his conscience: *"Thou shalt not covet"*. Guilty.

He envied the Joneses. He coveted what they had. Guilty.

St Paul admitted that it was this sin which nailed him as part of the sinful human race. Is there anyone anywhere who is not Guilty of envying the Joneses,

who is not guilty of coveting? (Reference: Letter to Romans chapter 7 verse 7)

**Do you envy others who have more 'stuff' than you do? _____**

**Do you feel that you are entitled to have their standard of living? _____**

***

# Capsule 20 Another Excuse For Greed "I Want To Live The Best Life"

*"I want to live the best life"*

"Best" is a wide-encompassing word that can embrace Quantity and Quality.

The "best life" is usually measured by the TV life-style show "Top Billing" standards, the enjoyment of living in luxury ....

residing in an immaculate Mansion, dining at expensive Restaurants, wearing Designer Fashion labels, visiting Exotic Locations.

Is that really 'the best' life?

Don't the inhabitants of those perfect palaces sometimes long for

a homely home where kids can be kids; leave things lying around in the bedroom?

a simple meal with the family around the kitchen table munching bread and Marmite?

a wardrobe of nice, comfy clothes, and if they get dirty Ma doesn't go ballistic?

a holiday in a time-share down at the beach where we know some locals by name?

The truly 'best life' enjoys simple things with occasional treats thrown in.

After all, regular everyday treats soon lose their treat-factor and become mundane.

Such treats are different only because they cost more than we should afford.

*The 'best life' is enjoyed only when the best Values are prioritised.*

Weaned from enslavement to Materialism, we can focus on Quality Values.

Listen to the Tributes at a Funeral: see how Values trump Material Success!

Seldom do the Tributes list all the material assets the deceased had accumulated.

All that was important while alive is now of no memorable value.

Instead, the mourners are reminded of the deceased Values:

His/her love, friendship, integrity, dependability, work ...... etc.

These sum up the truly "best life".

Here, on the next page, is a more comprehensive list of ... Values ...

**Values:** for example (in random order) ....

Hard Work,

a Good Work Ethic,
Learning & Earning,
Honesty,
Accountability
Dependability
Helpfulness.
Integrity,
Compassion for Others,
Kindness,
Sexual Purity,
Service,
Family,
Loyalty.

Note: These Values are important in all areas of our lives: our personal, work, recreational, community, family, economic, religious, social and national life. Resist the temptation to compartmentalise Values as if some only operate in defined areas.

Aim to be a person of Integrity, for whom the whole of life is integrated in unity.

The 'best life' is enjoyed only when the best Values are prioritised.

Weaned from enslavement to Materialism, we can focus on Quality Values.

*Do you define your "Best Life" ~ in Material Value? or in Quality Value terms?*

\*\*\*

# Capsule 21 Excuses for Greed Related To My Self-Esteem

Every person on earth has a deep longing to be loved, valued and appreciated.

Whether admitted or not, for some, this longing is at the top of their "Need List".

Wikipedia explains that 'Self-esteem' reflects a person's overall emotional evaluation of his or her own worth. It is a judgement of oneself as well as an attitude toward the self. Self-esteem is the positive or negative evaluation of the self, and how we feel about ourselves.

For some, their Material assets are a major factor in defining their personal worth, to themselves and to others. They will say:

*"My worth is measured by my wealth"*

After all, isn't that how we do our shopping? Good quality is more expensive. We have an automatic suspicion of anything that is inexpensive. In the long run, a cheaper item will turn out to cost us more in maintenance or replacement than a more expensive item. This truism is captured in the Afrikaans proverb "Goedkoop is duurkoop" ~ 'Cheapness is expensive'.

It is easy to transfer this to our personal worth. We even use the same word "worth" to describe a person's total assets: "I am worth R1.2 million". But if she didn't have any material assets at all, would this mean she was worthless? Never! She can still be a valuable Mother to her children, Wife to her husband, Cook in her kitchen, Cashier at work, Volunteer at Hospice, Sunday School teacher at Church. Those are service-Values that make her priceless.

But deeper than that is her personal Character. A person of Integrity, who can be trusted to keep her word, a kind and generous woman, one who exercises self-control, clean-living, and a lady who pays attention to her health. There are many positive characteristics that increase her Worth immeasurably. So what if she doesn't have a large personal bank-balance? She has a high personal Worth-Value.

**Contrast** her with another who is enormously wealthy. He drives an arrogant bull-barred SUV, dresses smartly, resides in an up-market gated suburb. He has made his money by wheeling and dealing, squashing his rivals, exploiting his staff, cheating the tax-man. He is selfish and stingy. A snob, with few real friends, but plenty of hangers-on hoping for some crumbs from the rich man's table.

What is his/her worth? By material standards, R900 million. By real standards, zilch. Actually s/he is a walking liability. S/he believes that "my worth is measured by my material wealth".

Her affluent life-style boosts her self-esteem. She is so boosted that she is arrogant. He is so inflated with the delusion of his own importance that he could burst at any moment.

*These extreme contrasts should stifle forever the idea that one's wealth is a valid measure of one's worth, one's self-esteem. Rather build your self-esteem on the strong foundation of your real worth, a worth that is measured by Character, Goodness and Lasting Values.*

If you find yourself thinking that

*"An affluent lifestyle will boost my self-esteem"*

face the reality that

*An affluent lifestyle can only boost an extremely hollow and fragile self-esteem.*

Don't slip into that Materialistic Temptation!

***

# Capsule 22 "I Suffered Under Apartheid, So Now It's My Time To Get Rich"

Chuck Stephens, Director of the Desmond Tutu Centre for Leadership NGO in Mpumalanga, in an email 12.5.2013, tells of a friend who gave him a valuable long-term background to this Excuse for the corruption and unaccountability that is becoming endemic:

> He said that, for about 40 years after the Anglo-Boer war, the British practiced corruption and unaccountability in South Africa. Not only blacks but whites of Dutch descent, were marginalized. Then from 1948 the Afrikaners, who had lost the war, won the peace. Apartheid was installed and for another 40 years, the Boers practised corruption and unaccountability. He grew up in this period as a boy of English descent. He said it was very open and frank that ONLY Afrikaners would occupy the upper eschelons of power. Others could get on with their private affairs, but were sidelined.

> His somewhat fatalistic view is that the same thing is now happening again. This time, it is the black ANC comrades who are in control. And they are having a heyday. They are feathering their own nests. They are (like goats in the African proverb) "eating where they are tethered". They are shameless about it. Opportunism reigns.

> (Chuck tells how) he recently consulted with an Advocate in the High Court about corruption. He warned that the way it was once seen - even by the courts - has changed. He

said that there are no longer absolutes - you are no longer just guilty or innocent. He said it is now relativistic - everyone is corrupt, so it is not fair for one judge to penalize offenders more than others have done. So the system is adjusting itself. It is going soft and rotten.

This week Tutu wrote that he was a strong supporter of the ANC during "the Struggle" against white minority rule. But citing inequality, violence and corruption, he stated that he would sadly not be able to vote for the ANC any longer. These are sharp words.

Nevertheless, I feel that his diagnostics are still working. Corruption is as big an enemy today as Apartheid was in the 1980s. The great problem with Triumphalism is that it tries to validate corruption with a simple retort: "It's our turn".

*(Quoted with permission)*

It is time for brave people of Integrity to have the courage to say "STOP! We will not pass this evil disease of Fraud and Corruption on to the next generation. We will draw the line now, so that our children will inherit a legacy of Integrity, and pass that on to their children."
We blame Colonialism and Apartheid for Corruption.
***Is that a sound reason to practice it ourselves?***

\*\*\*

# Capsule 23 Another Excuse: I Am Worth More Than I Am Being Paid

*(A Retiree tells how he fought this temptation)*

"Let me confess that this has been my strongest temptation. This is my story of how, after a lifetime of Contentment with a modest income, the Jealousy temptation hit me hard.

In my first real job, as a Life Assurance Assessor for the Old Mutual, I was satisfied with my remuneration of 27 pounds sterling a month. That was in 1955, and this was a reasonably good salary for a starter. Some of my peers earned less. Within three years I earned 32 pounds pm (=R64 in South Africa's later currency). But God had put a missionary calling on my life, and when I had saved enough to pay for full-time residential Bible College fees, I resigned. My employer tried to coax me to stay on by offering =R70 per month, but I stuck to my decision.

Eventually, after graduating from Bible College, I married and began service at a rural Mission station in the then-Transkei, living in a mud-brick house with long-drop toilet, no plumbing, no electricity. Our stipend was R35 p.m. each, less than half of what commerce was paying. Our contract did not promise a guaranteed stipend, and some months the money wasn't there. We were also prohibited from going into debt. (We took the cue, and have never been in debt since then - even to buy a home, or a car.) 14 months later we became parents, and bought our first car for R700 cash.

Later we were assigned to lecture at a Bible College. Our stipend increased with inflation but was still way below what our friends in the business world earned. I felt jealous when a colleague in an American mission received R1000 p.m. ("why do they get so much money?"). But I reminded myself that I had accepted a career that had given advance notice it would under-pay me. My job-satisfaction was extremely rewarding, serving Jesus by serving people.

Later I worked for an non-profit organisation as its CEO, where I could set my own salary as long as I was able to fund-raise this, together with its running expenses. Here I learned how to accomplish a lot on a shoe-string budget. Every trip, every project, had to cover its own expenses. A Value, derived from my missionary background, took root: I must sacrifice for a Cause that is greater than I am.

I travelled on the cheap, sometimes using public transport, dependent on local hospitality in suburb, township and informal settlement. In those apartheid years this opened my white eyes to realise that my salary, though low, was princely among many of my compatriots. If I felt hard done by, how much more must the less-privileged feel when comparing their income with mine?

The big Jealousy Test came when my organisation merged with another group, but the salaries stayed the same. I had major national responsibilities, yet was paid 30% less than the lowest paid in the other group. This educated me: Now I felt like most blacks had felt under apartheid's inequalities. To feel this injustice fuelled those jealousy temptations I had been fighting: "I have a responsible position, and I'm worth more than I'm being paid".

God reinforced my Values, and held me to them even when my health cracked under the strain of these tensions. I resigned, and there was a modest 'settlement'. But this experience has a happy ending: Some years later I received a letter from my ex-boss apologising for the way he'd treated me and asking forgiveness. I pay tribute to his grace, a reflection of the greater Grace of Jesus Christ which has supplied ALL our needs in life - and some treats as well. Even though we've always earned far below what most people regard as 'a decent living wage'" *(By permission)*.

***

# Capsule 24 Others Get Paid More Than I Am Paid

We work for the same boss. We do the same, or similar work. We carry the same responsibilities. Yet because I'm a woman and he's a man, he gets paid more than I am. Because she is White and I am Coloured, she gets paid more than I am paid. Because I'm a refugee from another country, I am exploited by being paid less than my colleagues who are local citizens.

The Constitutional Bill of Rights clauses 9 (3), 8 (2) require that there be no unfair discrimination on the bases of *inter alia* gender, race, ethnic or social origin. Yet there are some employers who do discriminate.

How do you handle this?

*Some of your Options are:*

a) Speak to your employer and try to negotiate a fair deal.

b) Seek help from a Trade Union - if one operates in your work-place.

c) Seek official help: Contact .....

**The CCMA, https://www.ccma.org.za/Contact**

**The Human Rights Commission,**
**https://www.bing.com/**
**search?q=Human | Rights+Commission+South+Africa+contact**

**The Commission for Gender Equality, http://www.cge.org.za**

Email: **cgeinfo@cge.org.za**


**The Black Sash**
   https://www.bing.com/search?q=black+sash+contact
   **Refugees    and    Asylum    Seekers**  should    consult
http://www.dha.gov.za/index.php/refugee-status-asylum


d) Change your job. Find an employer who will treat you fairly. Of course, with the current high unemployment rate, this is risky. It is wise to find a new job before resigning the old job.


e) Grin and bear it.

***But be sure you will NOT take the most Tempting Options: Fraud or Corruption.*** It is easy to rationalise this by saying to yourself "I'm only reimbursing myself for what my employer owes me." Don't sell your soul so cheaply. Having made your commitment to Integrity, don't renege now under the pressure of temptation.

***

# Capsule 25 Perceived Injustice (Perhaps the Most Subtle Excuse Of All)

*"I'm being treated unjustly"*

This Temptation has greater force if we know ***we are* "*better*** than the Joneses",

> we are more qualified, we have more experience, we are more productive ...
> and we ***deserve*** more than they have.

We tell ourselves that ***it is Unjust*** that they should be paid more than we are paid,

> or that they have got more 'stuff' than we have. And we believe what we tell ourselves ~
>
> so much so, that we are willing to be unjust in order to get justice!

The extra power of this Excuse is derived from its appeal to the high Virtue of Justice. Other excuses appeal to our baser instincts ... Greed, Envy and Jealousy.

> This Excuse disguises our ugly Greed with the noble virtue of Justice.
> Somehow Fraud and Corruption seem less serious in this disguise.

But with whatever the excuse we rationalise it, Fraud is Fraud, Corruption is Corruption.

> The end does not justify the means.

It is a lie to say *"Let us do evil that good may result"*
(Paul's Letter - Romans 3:8)

### How can you handle this Injustice with Integrity?

- Discuss your concerns with your boss, and ask for a just remuneration. Be confident and humble, presenting your case factually (not emotionally) Be willing to listen to the other side of the argument: Maybe you are wrong!
- If injustice persists, seek allies who can assist you: eg. Trade Union or Lawyer.
- If all else fails, bear the injustice with patience and dignity!

Remember: Fraud is a Temptation to be resisted.
Don't compromise your integrity.

### And never ever in a thousand years consider the Option of Fraud or Corruption.

*"What good is it for a man to gain the whole world, yet forfeit his soul? Or what can a man give in exchange for his soul?"* (Mark 8:36,37) Why should you damn your own soul to get even with your boss who is damning his soul by his sinful injustice? You are worth more than he is ~ don't stoop to that level. You don't have to wallow in the mucky sewage just because others do.

No matter how unjustly YOU are treated, make sure that YOU treat everyone else with Justice.

### When you are the Victim of Injustice, remember.... JUDGEMENT DAY IS COMING!

No-one but no-one gets away with Injustice forever.

One day the God of Justice will execute Final Justice!

### 23c The Song Of Final Justice

2 Corinthians 5:10 Revelation 20:10,12

*On the Judgement Day of Jesus, when the Judge takes up His place on His throne, the nations gathered trembling at His awesome face; Then God's Justice of all ages will be clearly seen and done; hidden evil manifested in the Light of God's own Son.*

Then the widow, crushed & beaten
by her landlord's greedy fist,
rises up to thank the Saviour
for His justice long-time missed.
Then the landless and exploited
by the powerful gravy train
riding heavy on their sorrows
start to sing with hope again.
Then the father robbed of justice
by some technicality
in a heartless legal system
finds God's judgment sets him free.
Mothers, children oft abused and
victims of their drunken men
now experience vindication
and a life of joy again.
And the pastor false accused of
stealing glory from the Lord,
using privilege for his pleasure,
while the Truth is being ignored.
Lies destroy his reputation,
former friendships melt away.
Yet he knows Truth will be told
on Jesus' Final Judgment Day.
Those who won't control their sex-drive,

careless of whom they infect
with the HIV pandemic,
sowing death with no respect
Rich men, who ignored the suffering
of the poor folk at their gate,
plead with God for drops of water
to relieve their judgment fate.
Terrorists and violent gangsters,
clerics who defraud the poor,
money launderers and fences
get the wage they've laboured for.
They'll receive eternal anguish,
while their victims are restored:
fully healed, restored, forgiven
as they trust in Christ their Lord.
Hear the multitudes acclaiming
justice that was long denied
now dispensed with truth and mercy
undistorted by self-pride.
Long the world has groaned in waiting
for this Day of God's own Son,
see His victory over evil,
praise His Kingdom fully come.

*Words: Hugh G Wetmore (c) September 2000*

*Chosen for the International Day of Prayer,*
*The Oval Stadium , Pietermaritzburg c. 2005*
*Metre 8787D*
*Tune: Austria ("Glorious things of thee are spoken")*

# Part Seven

# Power (Including conflict of interest)

# Capsule 26 The Power Of Power

Three Excuses depend on *the Power factor* for their popularity:

*"If I had more money I'd have more power"*

*"I can use my power to get more money"*

*"I have been given my position of power, and so why not use it for my benefit?"*

Power and Money go together. Money and Power reinforce each other. If you haven't yet got Power, you are hungry for it. It will open doors of infinite opportunity to get rich quick.

If you already have Power, you have the means to use that Power for your own economic benefit.

Power can be a drug to the mind and soul. It easily blurs the normal moral distinctions between right and wrong. Once you have tasted the Power of Power, you want more and more of it. You will do anything to maintain your power. Integrity doesn't matter ~ power becomes your all-consuming ambition.

Yes, Power can make your rich financially. But material benefits aside, pure naked power is its own reward. It feeds the Ego, your self-importance swells with pride. Power is addictive.

Hence the wheeling and dealing in the arenas of Power: Politics at every level, Corporate institutions, Sports administration, Financial institutions, Big Church Leadership.

A local church leader went overseas to be interviewed for an international leadership post. He was the only candidate. Before the deliberations began, leaders from other countries were lobbying him with their petitions, as if he had already been appointed. In the end, he was not appointed. But he had briefly tasted the intoxication of Power. It was an addictive feeling to bask in such international importance.

These are the tempting dynamics that surround positions of Power and Influence. It takes a humble spirit of sacrificial service to resist the temptation to Pride that so readily accompanies Power.

Once you have tasted Power and experienced its mesmerising addiction, it is so easy to slip into temptations of Corruption. A position of personal Power provides the Opportunity for Corruption.

That is why Politicians and Police are the most vulnerable to Corruption (according to Transparency International's International Barom eter, 2013). They have Power. The constable holding the Fine-book at the road-block has more power than the Director of Companies sitting in the car that has passed on a solid line. Youth and experience don't matter: The uniform and the badge confer Power. Power over everyone. Official Power that can be used for personal benefit.

I was once flagged down in the centre of Thohoyandou, capital of the then-Venda Homeland. The officer pulled out his fine-book. "What for?" I asked. "Stopping in a no-stopping zone" he replied. "But you told me to stop" I replied, "and where is the sign that says I can't stop here?" "You should know that this is a no stopping zone" he said. Realising I was being set up for a bribe, I drove away. I knew I had not committed an offence. He had the power, and he was using it for self-enrichment.

Power is a necessary tool with which to lead, to manage or to govern. But it is dangerous. Like dynamite, it is needed for mining or road-construction, but it must always be handled with care.

Don't let it explode in your hands by yielding to Corruption-temptation. Use Power for the benefit of Others, not for yourself. **See Capsule 28.**

Never allow yourself to be caught between Two Powers: The Power of your Position and the Power of your Purse. Otherwise your Purse will dictate to you the decisions your Position confers on you. You will use your Position to enlarge your Purse. This happens when you have an interest in a Company that is tendering for a contract. A contract that your Position empowers you to grant. Choose one or the other - never both. Declare your financial interest in the Company. Excuse yourself from deciding on the Contract. Avoid like the plague any Conflict of Interest.

***

# Capsule 27 The Hard Fight For Integrity In The Commercial World

*(A story of a Vain Fight against small-scale Abuse of Power)*

"In 2008, upon the sudden death of the previous Chairman, I was asked to take over the Management of a large Residential property. Thrown in at the deep end, I worked hard to familiarise myself with the task before me, and with the Sectional Titles Act which controlled this responsibility. With the help of a fellow-Trustee who had business-management experience, we sorted the boxes of papers and set up a workable filing system. We drew together a happy team of Trustees with strong competencies and experience. Soon the administration hummed efficiently. It was hard work, demanding an average of 30 hours a week, and on call 24/7. The pay was R1600, rising to R2600 over three years.

Our policy was to manage by the book (the Act), enforce the House Rules fairly and consistently, and listen to complaints and input from those we served and to whom we were accountable. Integrity was a treasured value, and when we made mistakes we admitted them with transparency. Consultants evaluated the aging building and the Owners voted for an extensive and expensive maintenance programme that required a drastic Levy-increase. With other creative initiatives our corporate income increased by nearly 30% pa. We began by re-waterproofing the roof. The increased income began to replenish our drained reserves.

At a time of low Reserves, an Owner used her right to attend Trustees' meetings to intentionally frustrate the smooth functioning of the administration. I offered her the Chairmanship, but she refused to even be a Trustee, because she wanted influence without responsibility. My health suffered, and I resigned.

Another Owner took over the Chair, and restructured the administration. All salaries were increased, two new posts were put in place. Almost all policies and procedures that we had carefully put in place were discarded. When we noticed how they were flouting the provisions of the Act and the House-Rules, and that the employed Caretaker was not fulfilling his Job Description, three of us ex-Trustees tried to interact courteously with the new administration. They would not listen, nor even reply to some of our letters. We were publicly accused of harassing them. We began to document all these instances of maladministration that could be proved in writing (ignoring the many verbal instances). We had proof of instances such as...

- The Chairman's refusal to acknowledge that the Sectional Title Act was legally binding.
- The Trustees policy to only apply the House-Rules at their discretion (=inconsistently).
- Many instances of not applying Rules re Overcrowding, Noise, Oil-leaks, Parking.
- The Chairman's assertion that Trustees could rule as they wished, no accountability.
- The Trustees certified that the AGM had approved their thirteen unilateral House-Rule amendments, though these had not been on the Agenda, nor in the AGM Minutes.
- Refusal to include a Motion to the AGM in the Minutes, yet recording 'it was defeated'.
- Chairman makes a personal profit of 813% for laminating, and 254% for photocopying.
- Minuted accusation "the previous Board 'made poor decisions leading to loss of funds'.
- 14 lies that contradict facts. e.g. "Washlines fixed weekly" - but broken for over a year. (If they can't be trusted in small matters, how can we trust them for anything?)

Eventually the Trustees invited us to meet with them to discuss our concerns. We agreed on the date and time, but 7 hours before starting time the Chairman cancelled the Meeting. We then made a Written Presentation (in lieu of the cancelled meeting), with a series of simple questions requiring Yes or No answers. They did not reply, but 2 months later we read their Minute declining to consider our Presentation. We didn't have the money to take them to Court, and we didn't have the emotional energy to continue flogging this corrupt horse."

**Comment:** The spirit of Dictatorship always lurks under the surface in any Organisation. Some people are so internally corrupt they don't know the difference between truth and lies, between right and wrong. They victimise those who try to hold them accountable. Jesus said: *"Don't throw your pearls to the pigs. If you do they will trample the pearls and tear you apart."* (Matthew 7:6)

\*\*\*

# Capsule 28 Using Power to Serve Others

We can easily become pessimistic when surrounded by examples of the Abuse of Power. But every day we come across stories of those who have Power, and unselfishly use it to serve Others. These deserve to be celebrated.

Successful Sports-people have Power. Many of them use it for the benefit of the under-privileged. Some Politicians use their Power for the benefit of the marginalised in Society. Yes, the cynics will say, this buys them votes. Of course, it is difficult to disentangle Motives, but we should give credit where credit is due:

Those Religious people, who have Power through earning a reputation of Integrity in service, are doing amazing deeds of compassion.

Think of Mahatma Gandhi, a Hindu, who led the revolution for the emancipation of India from colonial rule from a platform of self-denial and poverty. Ever since he has been praised as a selfless leader who chose to live in poverty to put the needs of others first, and used his power to advance the needs of the powerless.

Think of the charity 'Gift of the Givers', led by Dr Imtiaz Sooliman, headquartered in Pietermaritzburg, South Africa. They have become internationally recognised as an impartial channel for sending medical and food assistance to those suffering from war and natural disasters. They are even trusted by some in terrorist organisations to mediate in hostage situations. (See Capsule 52)

Think of Billy Graham and Samaritan's Purse charitable organisation. When, due to age, he had phased out of his international evangelistic service, a TV documentary investigated his rare level of Integrity. His powerful influence with presidents and world leaders was due to his moral stature. Samaritan's Purse distributes aid to deserving causes throughout the world. (See Capsule 50)

Think of Archbishop Desmond Tutu who, amid the swirling tides of public opinion, has earned a reputation for standing steadfast and true to his moral principles. Even those who disagree with him cannot say that he used his Ecclesiastical and Nobel Laureate power for selfish gain.

The greatest example is Jesus Christ. He had the ultimate power of Deity. No-one inherently had more intrinsic power than He had, as the omnipotent, sovereign God. Yet he taught and lived by the maxim:

*"Whoever would be great among you must be your servant. Even (I) the Son of Man came not to be served, but to serve, and to give his life as a ransom for many"* Mark 10:43

Jesus reprimanded His own followers who were power-hungry, seeking high status in His own Kingdom. He intentionally contrasted this use of Power with the abuse of Power prevalent among the rulers and leaders of the world (Mark 10:35-45).

He taught and modelled the reality that to have Integrity, and to use 'power' and 'influence' to serve the good of others, will lead to suffering - not popularity. He would take up His cross, and carry it outside the city of Jerusalem. There He would be nailed to that cross, and then lifted high on that cross, enduring the public shame of a criminal's execution. There He would *give his life as a ransom for many"*. He would carry our sins in His own innocent body, and bear the death-penalty that the rest of us deserve.

That is the price Jesus would pay for loving Integrity, an Integrity that ran counter to the popular twisted culture of the world.

Because of twisted human nature, those who use their Power and Influence to serve others, and not themselves, can expect opposition from those who see Power and Influence as a means to selfish ends. People who are 'twisted' resist being 'straightened'.

## 7k TWISTED THORNS

Lord of Integrity,
without deceit or guile,
Jesus, in whom was found no sin,
when He was put on trial,
He always spoke the truth,
His 'Yes' was always 'Yes',
exposed the world's hypocrisy,
Integrity He blessed.
He shone the light of truth
in darkened human hearts,
who then reacted angrily,
embarassed by their farce.
They tried to twist His word
in convoluted ways,
and tied themselves in hopeless knots
before His piercing gaze.

Their twisted evidence
revealed their twisted minds,
hell-bent on proving Jesus' guilt
by every means they find.
Till finally He tells
the truth just like it is,
that He's the Son of Man who comes
to judge, as Scripture says.
"Blasphemy" shouts the priest,
and Jesus is condemned
for telling Truth just like it is:
integrity offends!

They searched to find a charge
that sticks in Roman law,
and found it in His claim
to be a King forevermore.

Twisting again the truth,
this 'treason' charge they hurled.
But Jesus said His kingdom
was not of this present world.

In Pilate's twisted mind
the Truth could not be known.
He vacillated, then pronounced
his verdict from his throne:

"Crown him with twisted thorns,
then flog Him, do not spare,
then take him out to Calvary
and crucify him there.

Then place a sign above
his crown of twisted thorns
proclaiming He's the Jewish King,
so everyone's informed."

That's how the Saviour died,
condemned by twisted men,
their sins confused their twisted minds, c
ould they untwist again?

Yes, Jesus can make straight
the crookedness of sin,
creating straight, new minds in those
who crown him as their King.

Crown Him with many crowns,
Christ Jesus on His throne,
The Saviour died and rose again,

will come back for His own!

He straightens twisted lives,
He forms integrity
so we may live in Truth like Him,
now and eternally.

*Words: Hugh G Wetmore © 2012*
*Metre: 6686D (DCM)*
*Tune: Diademata ('Crown Him with many crowns')*

If you feel trapped by the temptation to Fraud and Corruption, tell Jesus about it. Admit your own twisted nature. Then ask Him to control your life, out of His own experience and ability to overcome twistedness, demonstrated on the cross.

# Part Eight

# Which temptations are strongest?

# Capsule 29 Which Temptations Are Likely To Conquer You?

*Go through this Check-list .... Know your Weak Points ....*
*Fortify yourself to resist*

**Without referring to Capsule 17 above, rate yourself again.**
*Rate your Vulnerability:*

5 = Irresistable Temptation; 4 = Strong Temptation; 3 = Modest Temptation 2 = Weak Temptation; 1 = Very Weak Temptation; 0 = No Temptation at all

- I don't want to let my Family down
- I want to give my kids the best start in life - they must have what others have o I am trying to keep up with the Joneses o I want to live the best life
- If I had more money I'd have more power
- I can use my power to get more money
- The affluent life-style boosts my self-esteem
- My worth is measured by my wealth
- I am being treated unjustly
- I am worth more than I am being paid
- Others get paid more than I do
- Nobody will know if I commit fraud
- I have been given my position of power, and so can use it for my benefit o I suffered before/under apartheid, so now it's my time to get rich o The opportunity is there, so why not take it?
- Other people are doing fraud and/or corruption, so why can't I?
- My boss is doing fraud and/or corruption, so if he fingers me I

can finger him
- Other people got away with it, so I can too

It's just a small amount

Remember your weak and vulnerable places,

the temptations which are most difficult to resist.

Set up special reinforcements at these places,

be aware that you could easily fall for these temptations.
Barricade these weak places with prayerful dependence on
God.

*"If you think you are standing firm, be careful that you don't fall! No temptation has seized*

*you except what is common to humanity. God is faithful; he will not let you be tempted beyond what you can bear. But when you are tempted, he will also provide a way out,*

*so that you can stand up under it."* 1 Corinthians 10:12,13

Commit yourself NOW to live a life of INTEGRITY,

and resist the Temptations to compromise your
INTEGRITY. Temptations will assault each of us in
different ways: BE PREPARED!

**Now compare your present ratings with your answer in Capsule 17.**

**Pay attention to your combined Strong points, and your combined Weak points.**

# Part Nine

# Motivation to Fight Corruption

# Capsule 30 We Need a Vaccine to Combat the Serious Pandemic of Fraud and Corruption

South Africa, indeed the world, is suffering an Pandemic of Fraud and Corruption. These evils are a highly contagious disease. It is possible that the warped minds of some greedy readers could use these examples to copycat their own fraud and corruption. This is the nature of the virus we are dealing with. It soon spreads till whole communities are infected.

The danger that this infective Pandemic can spread demands that drastic decisions be made. The nation ~ politicians and professionals, priests and preachers, the powerful and the poor ~ all must be resolute is their determination to stamp it out.

Prior to the 1950s, Poliomyelitis was a serious threat to people, especially children. Many died, many more were permanently disabled by polio. Then the Salk vaccine was invented, and a drop of this miracle liquid on each child's tongue bequeathed immunity to the whole world. Within a generation, polio was eradicated. Today this is almost an obsolete disease.

We need a vaccine to immunise people against the temptation to Fraud and Corruption.

This epidemic is rapidly getting out of hand. It is perpetuating poverty.

Poverty is the universal consequence of a society riddled with fraud and corruption. The rich get filthy rich. The poor live in filthy poverty. Fraud & Corruption are filthy diseases.

If we could immunise the world against fraud and corruption, we would eradicate the world's poverty within a generation.

*INTEGRITY is the moral 'Salk vaccine'*

*that will strengthen the immune systems of individuals bombarded with the infection of Fraud and Corruption.*

## WE NEED STRONG MOTIVATION TO APPLY THE INTEGRITY VACCINE...........

Enthusiasm for Integrity

Anger at all that sabotages Integrity

A Passion for Social Justice

Compassion for the Poor

A tender Conscience

Stubbornness to persevere for Integrity

Courage to expose it wherever it manifests

Anger at Fraud and Corruption

***

# Capsule 31 Motivated By Anger

Why don't people act against the pandemic of Fraud and Corruption devouring Society?

Because not enough people get Angry!

And when people do get angry, they are not Angry enough!

It is easy to blame Society in general for not getting Angry about Fraud and Corruption.

But each of us must ask ourselves:
"Am *I* really angry enough about Fraud and Corruption?"

People are quick to take action when they are angry enough.

When they gather on a hill in Marikana, armed with weapons, motivated by anger.

When they block the highways with rocks, protesting bucket sanitation.

When they burn the vineyards because they get paid too little.

When they rampage as an alleged rapist gets bail.

When they destroy schools because of no tarred road.

Riots ~ rational or irrational ~ are sparked when the masses are angry.

Anger becomes a negative, emotive motivation when it is irrational and uncontrolled.

Anger destroys clinics and libraries, and kills people, when it becomes hysterical.

On the other hand, controlled Anger, carefully considered, can be a force for Good. Constructive Anger directed against Evil is a positive motivation,

a motivation that can effect healthy change for the Good of everyone.
As the following true story demonstrates:

*A man of peace* stood watching the goings-on in the city market.

He walked among the vendors, looking, listening and contemplating their activities.

He saw exploitation, over-pricing, profiteering, monopolistic money-changing.

He felt the frustration as the destitute were milked of their savings.

But it was getting late. He went to his lodgings and brooded over what he had seen.

The more he considered, the more angry he became. He couldn't ignore it.
But, as a good man, a man of peace, he kept his anger under control.

The next day, full of controlled anger, he made a whip, then entered the market-place.

Brandishing his whip he chased the vendors from their stalls.

He over-turned the money-changers' tables, scattering their money on the floor.

But what really fuelled the anger of this man of peace was the *Venue* for this city-market.

The traders had hi-jacked the wide, open court-yard of *the Temple* for their business.

This was the Temple dedicated to the worship of the one true God.

But they were worshipping the idol of Money, not God.
They were motivated by Greed, not Generosity.

God, to whom this Temple was dedicated, was a God of Love, Mercy and Justice.

They were violating the Values of God, and venerating the Values of Satan.

And those who didn't know the true God got a totally warped view of Him.

This Man of peace was Jesus of Nazareth, Messiah.

Divinity personified - temporarily living as a human being among us here on earth. He justified his actions: *"My house shall be called a house of prayer for all nations ~*

*but you have made it a den of thieves"* (Gospel of Mark 11:11,15-17)

If this Man of Peace, Jesus Christ, could vent his controlled anger

against the idolatry of greed that fuelled the economic exploitation of the poor, then surely we should have the courage to vent our controlled anger against the fraud and corruption which are exploiting the poor today.

**On a scale of 1 (no Anger) to 10 (extremely Angry) ~ how angry are you at fraud and corruption?** _____

# Capsule 32 Get Angry ~ Because Corruption Deepens Poverty

Nigeria's rulers, from independence in 1960 to 1999, stole or misused 220 billion pounds sterling (about R2.6 trillion), a sum equivalent to 300 years of British aid for the entire continent of Africa. Just one military dictator, General Sani Abacha, stole between one and three billion pounds during his 5-year rule. This mass theft left two-thirds of the country's 130 million people ~ one in seven of the total African population ~ living in abject poverty. A third is illiterate, and 40% have no safe water supply. (Sunday Times 26.6.2005) *Be angry!*

Every month desperate miners' widows whose pensions have dried up, make the long haul from Mozambique, Malawi, Lesotho and Zimbabwe to the offices of the Mineworkers Provident Fund in Johannesburg to find out where their money is. But each time they leave empty-handed. They are victims of the Fidentia collapse that saw R1.47 billion of widows' and orphans' money disappear. Some have had to borrow money for the trip. One of them, Maria (42), a mother of seven, has already made 3 trips from Lesotho to Gauteng, each costing R1000, but returns empty-handed each time. "When I complained that I could not afford the trip home, they said they were not interested. Why do they treat us like this?" she asked. Where is the money they invested? Millions were spent by Fidentia in buying out other businesses, and in funding the high life of Fidentia's bosses, it was claimed. NUM says it is upset by what has happened. (Pretoria News 7.7.07)

*Be angry at this selfish Greed!*

"KZN MEC's Luxury cars show contempt for the poor" commented Linda Aadnesgaard, Director of the Thandanani Association Aids Orphans Programme and Abandoned Children's Project. "Education and Culture MEC Eileen kaNkosi-Shandu spends

R23 408 per month on her vehicles, Premier Lionel Mtshali R20 000 pm, and Public Works MEC Celani Mthethwa R16000 pm. We are continuously told that there is no money for caregivers of children other than the paltry (1999 rate) R100 per child per month (to the age of 7). This MEC travel money could supply thousands of children with child support grants. We are sick of this hypocrisy." When the ACDP's Jo-Anne Downs queried the spending of R260 000 on MEC's vehicles over 8 months, the Leader of the Legislature, Blessed Gwala called her "a political prostitute" and "the most racist member he had encountered". (Witness 6.8. and 3.9.99). Playing the Race Card and Name-calling aggravates anger at this evil. *Such profligate spending of our tax-money on personal luxury to the neglect of the poor must make us angry.*

The former Welfare Minister, Geraldine Fraser-Moleketi failed to spend R200 million of a R204 million Poverty Relief allocation between 1997 and 1999. The money was allocated to assist the poor, but it was not used. It was those living in abject poverty who suffered, while those who failed to do what they were well-paid to do, lived in luxurious comfort.

(Witness 18.3.2000). Of R100 million allocated in 1996/7 to ease the plight of 30 000 victims of violence, only R12 million was used. (Witness 24.8.1999) *Be angry!*

School Principal Sylvester Buthelezi was convicted of fraudulently stealing R135 000 from Dept of Health funds for feeding-scheme projects for the underprivileged in the Uhombo district between 1993 and 1996, and was ordered to repay the stolen money. He lost his appeal against his conviction and the 4 year prison sentence; but the high court ruled that the regional court had erred in requiring him to repay the stolen sum! (The Mercury 18.6.99) *Be angry - and cry over the injustice of the law!*

Welfare officials plundered the poor in KwaZulu-Natal by nullifying payments to legitimate grant recipients, and taking the money for themselves. 25 000 cases of fraud have been uncovered, involving R71 million. (W itness 26.2.2003) Three years later another scandal was reported: Of the 300 000 of South Africa's 11.5 million Welfare Grants that were cancelled due to fraud, 12 000 were being claimed by government officials. By weeding out these fraudulent claimants, government saved R1.2 billion in the year to March 2006. More than 2000 civil servants have so far agreed to repay grants. (W itness 20.5.06)

*Be angry when those with jobs and adequate salaries rob the jobless destitute!*

 **Now....... On A Scale Of 1 (No Anger) To 10 (Extremely Angry)**

 ~

 **How Angry Are You At Fraud And Corruption?**

 ———

***

# Capsule 33 Get Angry When Corruption Feeds Off Suffering

When the COVID-19 Pandemic circled the world with its deadly infection, Governments and Civil Society everywhere tackled the virus with every possible strategy. Millions of innocent people suffered. The infection rate soared, and hundreds of thousands died of Covid-related diseases. The scary feature of this Corona Virus was that some who had no symptoms were nevertheless infecting others, who got the symptoms - some of them fatally.

In March 2020, after the first local cases were diagnosed, South Africa declared a State of Disaster. A hard Lock-down restricted people to their homes, and only essential businesses were allowed to operate. Their slogan was *"We must save Lives"*. As the Lockdown restrictions were gradually lifted, we realised that many businesses had closed, and millions were out of work. Poverty was rampant. Relief measures were put in place. And a new slogan appeared: *"We must save Lives and Livelihoods"*. Now only a few classes of business were prohibited. One of these was an alcohol ban, which did miracles in emptying the hospitals' trauma wards, and in reducing traffic accidents. Lives were saved, but not the livelihoods of those earning their incomes from the alcohol trade. The State had a tricky balancing act to manage.

To protect the medical staff from being infected by their Covid-patients, they were supplied with Personal Protective Equipment (PPEs). Over 1200 contracts to supply PPEs to the Gauteng Health Department were signed, totalling R30,7 billion. The Special Investigating Unit was alerted to possible corruption, and it investigated contracts worth R13,3 billion.

In the SIU's Report on 5th February 2021 they found "corruption on an unprecedented scale". One contractor was interviewed, who admitted that he had only registered his company the day before the

State of Disaster was proclaimed, that he had no experience in PPEs, and that he did not have the capital to start his company. The Health Department had paid him in advance, but he had not yet delivered on the contract worth millions. The Report said that there was a pattern of "over-paid and under-delivered". "There appeared to be political pressure in the granting of contracts, which had not followed due procedures." The Gauteng Minister of Health and his wife, the President's Spokesperson, were fingered.

How deep is the moral delinquency of both the Health Department and the Tenderers, hat they should make unjust profit from the misery of this pandemic! Contrast this attitude with that of Dr Imtiaz Sooliman, founder of the Gift of the Givers charity managing billions of Rands in gifts from the public, who said:. "I have no desire for clothes. I have no desire for holidays. I have no desire for outings. **All I see is the suffering of people**... I have no pension plan, because I don't have much earnings..."

Get Angry when you see corrupt government and businesses feeding off the sufferings of the people. Get Angry, very Angry!

**NOW ....... On a scale of 1 (no Anger) to 10 (extremely Angry)**

~


**How Angry Are You At Such Fraud And Corruption?**

_____


***

# Capsule 34 Controlled Anger Must Lead To Controlled Action

Anger that is uncontrolled leads to anarchy.

Action that is uncontrolled *is* anarchy.
Anarchy destroys a community, and eventually a Nation.
We do NOT want to go down THAT road.

That is why our Anger must be controlled, disciplined anger.

Make sure that all Anger is under the control of your Rational Mind, that it is geared to a constructive Strategy.

A Strategy that will deal with Greed. Fraud and Corruption.

A Strategy that will promote Integrity.
A Strategy that will strengthen Immunity to the Temptation to Dishonesty.

\*\*\*

As we Control our Anger, and as we Control our Action, we can implement a wise Strategy.

The Emotion of Anger is the Fuel that drives our Action against Fraud and Corruption.

This Action is Controlled and Directed by the Steering of our Rational Mind.
Let's begin now to use our Rational Mind in forming a Wise Strategy:.
Think. Think carefully.

All acts of Fraud and Corruption, all Theft and Deceit, are committed by *People*.

*You* are one of those people who is capable of committing these evils.

Don't be deceived into thinking "*I'll* never do crime". We are all vulnerable. As the saying goes "Every person has their price".

Given the right circumstances, pressures, desires and opportunity

....

I can be tempted.
I can give in to Temptation.
I can do Fraud and Corruption.

What Strategy can I find that will strengthen my Immune Resistance to such Temptations?
The first step in Strategy Development is to ask:
**What Pre-Conditions must be Present**

**for Anyone to be Tempted to Fraud and Corruption?**

Then we must ask:
**What is the *Source* of Temptation to Fraud and Corruption?**

# Part Ten

# Downsizing Greed to Contentment

# Capsule 35 Economics 101: Look Before You Leap

Economics is a major driver of political foolishness as well. Observe how democratic
Governments tend to work:
Politicians go out into the Community and promise the people just what they want.

The voters believe them, and vote for the Party that makes the nicest promises.

When the winning Party is in Government, the politicians realise they don't have the money to fulfil their promises.

The voters then, rightly, get angry and they, wrongly, riot, destroying the infrastructure they already have. Now they are worse off than they were before.

The wiser way would be for the Government to know how much money it has, and then only promise the people what it can afford. But then, of course, the governing Party would not be voted into power again, because voters vote on the basis of the Promises! So the voters expect the Government to fulfil its promises - which it can't. So the anger and rioting continues its vicious cycle, until ... the country lies in ruins.

*Why, oh Why, are the voters so gullible?*
   *Because that's the way they manage their own lives.* I generalise:
They buy according to their wants and desires. They do not first draw up a budget to know what they can afford. Like the Government, they

promise themselves what they want. But when they can't pay for what they have wanted and bought, they .............. are in debt.

Soon they discover that debt is expensive. They need more money than they've got, to pay the installments. The unpaid installments get added to the original capital debt. They owe more and more. So the debt-spiral drags them ever downwards.

Maybe this is what the apostle meant when he wrote about: *"a trap and many harmful and foolish desires that plunge men into ruin and destruction"* (1 Timothy 6:9).

It is the Human Habit to follow the Heart rather than the Head. You've noticed how many people marry on the basis of 'having feelings for him/her'. Feelings come and feelings go. When this Human Habit sees the advertisement, or walks down the aisles of the supermarket, Feelings of the Heart are dominant. Purchases are made. Only when the credit-card statement arrives, does the Head begin to ask "How will I pay for this???"

**Wise people 'Look before they Leap'.**

> **Look carefully at the Affordability before Leaping into the transaction.**

> **Don't Leap into the transaction before Looking at the Affordability.**

> **If you Leap before you Look, don't ask later 'Why did I get hurt?'**

By exercising this Wisdom, you'll never fall into the Temptation to Fraud and Corruption.

Instead, your personal financial situation will give you a deep sense of CONTENTMENT.

Contented people don't fall into the Greedy love of Money which can lead to Corruption

***

# Capsule 36 How To Downsize Greed

1. Face the fact that Corruption is driven by Greed. Without Greed, there would never be Corruption.

1. Face the fact that Greed is comfortably nestling in your own heart.

You find yourself longing for "things".
You think you'll be happier if you have them.
You would not be so happy if you did not have them.
You ask yourself: "If s/he can have it, why can't I?"

1. Face the fact that you could become Corrupt, if the opportunity presents itself.

1. Review your replies to Capsule 31: *Which temptations are likely to conquer you?*

**WHICH TEMPTATIONS ARE LIKELY TO CONQUER YOU?**
*Go through this Check-list .... Know your Weak Points .... Fortify yourself to resist*

Refer to your answers in Capsules 17 and 29 for this personalised summary

Write down in the space below, **your five most powerful temptations-to-Corruption:**
1.
2.
3.
4.
5.

Commit yourself (in writing) to some clear steps you will take to downsize Greed in your own heart/mind.

1.

2.

3.

4.

5.

***

# Capsule 37 Your Enemy Is Also Examining Your Weak Points

In the previous Capsule Thirty you've done some serious introspection.

Visualise your life as a game where you are trying to win for Integrity.

You are the Coach of your life, working to improve your life-game.

You have identified your strong points in life's game of Integrity.
You have also identified your weak points, where you could easily fail.

Your Assistant Coach has the happy name of "Contentment".

Contentment is invaluable in winning the life-game of Integrity.
Without Contentment you will lose the game.

"Contentment" is an invisible Value of satisfaction with life and what it throws at you.

It is not a slave to visible things, which many people think are most important.

///////oooOooo\\\\\\\
The opposing side in the Game is coached by the devil.

His aim is to oppose Integrity at every point, causing you to fall into Dishonesty.

When you are dishonest, it is easy to do Fraud, and become Corrupt.

The devil's Assistant Coach has the sad name of "Greed".

His surname is "Materialism" ... so what is that?

"Materialism" is a life-habit of concentrating on visible Material things.

rather than the invisible Values OF Character and Integrity.

As the Coach of the opposing team, the devil loves watching videos of your life.

He studies your game plan, looking for your weak points, so he can exploit them.

He was looking over your shoulder as you completed the previous Capsule 30.

His assistant Coach, Greedy Materialism, always has some strategic Moves in mind, temptations that will defeat you, if you are not wide-awake.

///////oooOooo\\\\\\\
So just HOW can you win this Life-game?

The way to avoid falling for his schemes is to *"be self-controlled and alert"* for *"your enemy the devil prowls around like a roaring lion*

*looking for someone to devour". So "resist him"* (1 Peter 5:8,9)

We are in a war-zone - while we want overcome temptations to Fraud and Corruption, our invisible enemy, the devil, is scheming to lead us into Fraud and Corruption.

A war is made up of many battles, and our desire is to win each temptation-battle, so that we will ultimately win the war.

*Are you committed to victory?*

If so, you need the help of assistant coach CONTENTMENT!

***

# Capsule 38 Contentment Instead Of Greedy Materialism

When you listen to the Pop-prophets of 'Success', you'll soon discover that they measure 'Success' in material terms. We noticed this earlier: A person is "successful" if they have accumulated Possessions. These are the ones who "have done well for themselves".

It doesn't matter whether they are nasty, selfish people. It doesn't matter whether they got their wealth through corruption (as long as nobody knows about it). It doesn't matter whether they discriminate against, or even oppress, others. They are deemed successful because they have a posh home, drive a top-of-the-range BMW and take overseas holidays every year.

Meanwhile, over there in a lower-class suburb lives a man who is happily married, rides a bicycle, and spends his annual leave pottering in his garden. He is cheerful and friendly to all his neighbours. Others would never say "he has done well for himself."

Yet, deep down, this man is CONTENT. He doesn't spend his waking hours comparing himself with the Joneses. He is not anxious because he lacks the expensive things of life. He enjoys spending time with his family and friends. He is grateful for occasional treats, and doesn't take them for granted. He has a home and enough food and clothing, and pays his bills on time. He is CONTENT.

Some people have been hoodwinked into believing those preachers who preach that they can "claim prosperity and wealth from God, because He wants you to be rich". Just "name it and claim it", they say. "The tongue has the power" (Proverbs 18:21). God wants you to have what you want. *Ask and you will receive* and it helps to tack on the phrase "in the name of Jesus" to your greedy prayers. And the high-flying lifestyles of those billionaire preachers seem to endorse this Prosperity teaching.

Such teachings were heard even in the early church. Paul warned against *"men of corrupt mind who have been robbed of the truth because they think that godliness is a means to financial gain"* (1 Timothy 6:5). The apostle urges the opposite: *"Godliness with CONTENTMENT is Great Gain"*. While the world foolishly rushes on in pursuit of "financial gain", even using their religion as a means to achieve it, the wise Christian sees how shallow and hollow that goal is. The wise person chooses to rather pursue the *"great gain of CONTENTMENT"* (1 Timothy 6:6).

If you have the basics of life, *"be CONTENT with that"* (1 Tim othy 6:8). You don't need all those flashy trimmings. Don't spend your energy, don't go into debt, for superfluous 'stuff' you don't really need.

In fact you are really worse off by going for greed, and neglecting CONTENTMENT. It is not being rich that is the root problem - it is to *"want to be rich"*. *"People who want to be rich fall into temptation and a trap. They fall into many foolish and harmful desires that plunge men into ruin and destruction"* (1 Tim othy 6:9). It is **the discontented wanting** to be rich that creates the problem. It is not **Money** that is the problem. It is "the **love** of money". Greed. Read verse 10: *"For the love of money is a root of all kinds of evil."* Almost every instance of Fraud and Corruption is triggered by *"wanting to be rich"*, by *"the love of money"*. This is the GREED which, given the right OPPORTUNITY, will trap you into Fraud and Corruption.

So what happens when you are "eager for money"? It can destroy you - in this life and the next. *"Some people, eager for money, have wandered from the faith and pierced themselves with many griefs."* (1 Tim othy 6:10). That's serious. Be warned! Avoid Greed. Never wander from the faith of Jesus Christ. Do not pierce yourself with many griefs. Don't take the risk. Being *"eager for money"* is a sure route to being Corrupt. Almost no-one has done Corruption who was not first *"eager for money"*.

**Whether you are a Christian or not,**

choose CONTENTMENT over Greedy Materialism.

\*\*\*

# Capsule 39 Choose To Pursue Nobler Goals Than Money

**This Resolution is for Everyone. But especially for Christians ... and even more especially for Christian leaders.** You do not have to be a Christian to avoid Corruption. But, if you are a Christian, you are obligated to overcome the temptation to Corruption.

How do you avoid Corruption in a world where so many citizens are greedy? They love money, and will do all they can to get more of it. They will even be corrupt to get money.

The answer is logical: Substitute nobler goals for the lower goal of greed for money. Note how 1 Timothy 6:11 supplies such a list of five "nobler goals" that will conquer corruption:

1. *"BUT you, man of God, flee from all this and pursue righteousness, godliness, faith, love and gentleness."* One does not kick a habit without embracing a substitute habit. If you want to *"flee"* the temptation to love money and be greedy, then pursue these opposite ethical goals:

   a) "Righteousness" = a right moral lifestyle, in contrast with a wrong
   moral lifestyle.

   This is wider than Contentment: it includes Integrity, Honesty, Sexual control, obeying the Law, and it relates to the following characteristics ...

   b) "Godliness" simply = Godli(ke)ness ... Godlikeness. Living the way God lives. Copying His ethics and character This will achieve the 'right moral lifestyle' in a) above.

c) "faith" = fixing your faith in Jesus Christ, who is totally worthy of your confident trust. Become a person of 'faith' follows Jesus Christ as His disciple or mentoree.

d) "love" = for God and others. As Christ loved us sacrificially; As we love ourselves. Denying ourselves for the sake of God and for the good of other people.

e) "gentleness" = being humble, not arrogant, proud, brash, holier-than-thou. It includes kindness and sensitivity to the different personalities of other people.

***Such a person will be unlikely to be Greedy, Love Money or fall for Corruption.***

1. *"Fight the good fight of the faith. Take hold of the eternal life to which you were called when you made your good confession in the presence of many witnesses"* (1 Tim othy 6:12). From this we learn ...

a) *"Fight the good fight of the faith."* Taking a stand against Greed, the love of Money, Fraud and Corruption is not for sissies. It's a "fight" that demands courage and persistent determination. It's not a three minute bout in the ring. It is a fighting War! There is plenty of opposition, because everyone loves Money and wants more of it. Corrupt colleagues don't like whistleblowers, and are ready to buy your silent cooperation. And it takes "faith" to believe that, even though there are setbacks, Jesus and His Lifestyle will win out in the end.

b) *"Take hold of the eternal life to which you were called "*. When we fight the faith-war against the love of money and corruption, we will also be aggressively grabbing eternal life and holding on to it. God has called us to the eternal life. This life is in God's Son Jesus (1 John 5:11,12). Eternal life is a 'quality' of life as well as a 'duration' of life. Materialism, the love of money, greed, corruption – these are temporary things

... the eternal life is forever. Take the long-term view: Fix you faith in Jesus, and fight these temporary evils.

c) *"You were called when you made your good confession in the presence of many witnesses"*. This refers to Timothy's public baptism, when he publicly announced that Jesus was Lord of his life, while simultaneously believing in his heart that God had raised the crucified Jesus from the dead. See Romans 10:8,9.

Yes, people may fight against the greedy love of money without having fixed their faith in Jesus and without the power of eternal life. And it is commendable when some do behave ethically.

But the Gospel calls all who have trusted Jesus to fight out their faith in an unselfish lifestyle, as a follower of Jesus Christ. By taking a public stand for Jesus you are obliged to fight Greed and Corruption in a spirit of material Contentment.

If you are a Christian with your faith in Jesus, then you are obliged to be CONTENT, and not to be enslaved by the greedy love of money.

It was Jesus Himself who said *"No one can serve two masters. You cannot serve (love) both God and Money"* (Matthew

6:24; Luke 16:13). So we make our choice: *"As for me and my household, we will serve the LORD"* (Joshua 14:15).

\*\*\*

# Capsule 40 Beware Of Consumerism

Everyone living in this 21 Century Culture is bombarded by Advertising that promotes

We can't be satisfied unless we have 'this latest gadget'.

We can't be beautiful unless we have 'this fabulous cosmetic'.

Our hunger demands 'this specific food'.

If we aren't hungry, then its our taste-buds which demand 'this tasty food'.

Our clothes are out of fashion without 'the best brands', so me must wear them.

Then ... We are not allowed to take time to think about their messages. No, the Special Offer is only valid TODAY. So we buy now and think later.

And ... We are not allowed to buy just one item ... "Buy three, and SAVE!" This is an effective advertising technique for those of us who want to 'save' ... and who doesn't?

So our Consumerism habit continues. An empty purse doesn't stop us. It's convenient to use the credit card, so we don't need to have the cash ahead of the purchase. And as someone said "A Bargain is something you don't need at an irresistible price"!

Also, Consumerism is good for the Economy. The Economy must keep spinning, for this is how jobs are created and sustained, and this is how people make a living. It's obvious:

The more we buy, the more they sell. So, many will argue, Consumerism is a good habit.

*A Case Study in a Case of Booze:* During the Covid-19 lockdown, the distribution and sale of alcohol was banned. Those businesses that were dependent on selling alcohol complained that they were going bankrupt, and thousands of jobs were being lost. This happened around New Year Celebration Party time. The demand for alcohol peaks at New Year. But all gatherings were banned, so those who can only have fun when sozzled were denied their annual Fun-Binge. Usually, the New Year drinking sprees kept the Trauma units in the hospitals full. Alcohol causes quarrels and violent fights which feed the hospitals with work to do. But now, with the sale and transport of alcohol banned, their trauma wards were empty, giving space for the increased Covid-admissions. When alcohol is mixed with driving, the accident rate is high. But now, without the alcohol factor, it dropped to the lowest ever.

BUT - Why are so many businesses and jobs dependent on something that causes so much suffering? 'Tis Economics that drives this crazy pleasure-provider. We're trapped. It doesn't make sense. Isn't it possible to create jobs and make money, without asking for grief and trouble as well? Or can we at least reduce the shameful consequences of the liquor industry? Ban its advertising, especially when linked to sport? More regulation?

# Part Eleven

# Exposing Corruption-Whistle Blowing

# Capsule 41 Exposing, Resisting Corruption

The 2013 "EXPOSED" campaign mobilised Christians throughout the world to sign a petition that would be presented to the G20 Summit of international economically influential countries. It urged strategies to quell the rising tide of Corruption. Their published Motivation can never become out-of-date in the war against Poverty.

**"Corruption has a name, poverty has a face, and you have a voice! You can add your voice to the 100 million Christians who are taking a stand against corruption.**

**Why should there be a global Christian campaign against corruption? According to the World Bank US$1 Trillion goes missing each year as a result of corruption across the globe. In Africa alone corruption costs the continent US$148 Billion. That is 25% of the total GDP of the continent.**

**These losses have a direct impact upon you and me. Corruption increases the cost of products and services ~ since the cost of bribes, or inflated prices, are passed on to consumers and taxpayers. Corruption also limits the development of infrastructure and services.**

**When corrupt business steal money from the government through colluding on tenders, not declaring their income, and not paying their taxes, less roads can be built, fewer schools can be supplied with teachers and resources such as books, hospitals are underfunded and understaffed, security and justice are undermined and our safety is put at risk. In some situations corrupt individuals cause an imbalance in justice in a nation – people with more money and influence don't get prosecuted for crimes and eventually the rule of law in a nation collapses.**

It is always the poorest members of society who suffer the effects of corruption most acutely. In some parts of Africa women must pay bribes to get basic medical support when giving birth to their babies. Some people won't have access to clean water because of incompetence and maladministration in local governments. Grants intended for the elderly, the sick, and the young may never reach their intended recipients, and so they will go without food, shelter and clothing.

Eradicating poverty

It is estimated that it would take just 1 per cent of the world's GDP to eradicate extreme poverty. In other words, we could ensure that every living person had enough food, clean water, sufficient medical assistance, and access to education. However, because of our greed, or because we do not act against those who are corrupt, very little is done to ensure that no one has too much while another person has too little.

What is clear is that it does not please God! In fact the Bible tells us to, *"Seek justice. Help the oppressed. Defend the cause of orphans. Fight for the rights of widows"* (Isaiah 1.17 NLT).

You can make a difference!"

# Part Twelve

# Values

# Capsule 42 A Clash of Values

In serving with a Christian Organisation, the staff experienced a sudden change of policy initiated by the CEO, and supported by the Chairman of the governing Board. All of the Values which had previously formed the basis of operation were suddenly superceded by a new Value imported from the national political correctness of the day: Affirmative Action, aka "Broad Based Black Economic Empowerment". One's Racial Identity became a more important qualification than Character or Competence.

This Organisation had pioneered Black advancement, and had gone against the Apartheid tide in the 1980s - flouting the Group Areas Act, and appointing Black management when this was NOT politically correct. Staff and students had protested and marched against Apartheid.

Now, in 2007, well into the Democratic era, the CEO arbitrarily demoted and/or fired all the white staff in favour of black replacements, at inflated salaries. Staff tensions were tight. A lobby from all racial groups opposed these moves. A Mediator diagnosed the issue as "a conflict of personalities", and urged Reconciliation. The lobby replied that the conflict existed at a deeper level: the level of Values. One cannot reconcile people with clashing sets of Values.

They drafted the following set of Values, which arose out of their core identity as Christians. They pleaded with the CEO to prioritise these Values above those of Race.

| | |
|---|---|
| LOVE vs Hatred | (1 Corinthians 13:4-6; 1 John 3:11-24) |
| HOLINESS vs Worldliness | (1 Peter 1:13-16; 1 John 2:15-17; Eph. 4:20-32) |
| CHRISTLIKENESS vs Satanlikeness | (Romans 8:29; 2 Corinthians 3:18; John 8:44) |
| INTEGRITY vs Hypocrisy | (Matthew 23; Psalm 15; 1 Corinthians 11:1) |
| TRANSPARENCY vs Secrecy | (1 John 1:7; Ephesians 5:8-14) |
| JUSTICE vs Injustice | (Genesis 18:19; Isaiah 61:8; Matthew 23:23) |
| COMPETENCY vs Incompetency | (1 Tim othy 3:2,5; Rom ans 12:5-8) |
| SELF-SACRIFICE vs Selfishness | (Luke 9:23-25; Galatians 5:20; James 3:14-16) |
| CONTENTMENT vs Greed | (Philippians 4:11-13; 1 Tim othy 6:5b-10) |
| FAITHFULNESS vs Unfaithfulness | (Luke 19:17; 1 Corinthians 4:2) |
| TEAMWORK vs Unilateralism | (1 Peter 5;1-3; 1 Corinthians 12) |
| ACCOUNTABILITY vs Independence | (2 Corinthians 5:9,10; Acts 5:1-11; 1 Corinthians 4:1-5) |
| EXCELLENCE vs Mediocrity | (Colossians 1:28,29; 3:17; 1 Thessalonians 2:12) |
| SEXUAL PURITY vs Sexual immorality | (Matthew 5:27-30; Ephesians 4:17-20; 1 Thess 4:3-8) |
| SEXUAL PURITY vs Sexual immorality | (1 Thessalonians 4:1, 3:6-15) |
| WORK vs Laziness | (2 Thessalonians 3:6-15) |
| HUMILITY vs Arrogance | (Luke 14:11; Philippians 2:3; Mark 7:22) |

In affirming these Values, the Lobby Group was being true to their Christian identity. They were demonstrating Integrity. Those who were prioritising their political/social agenda were squashing their Christian Values in favour of the Values of the world in which we live. They lacked Integrity. They evidenced Hypocrisy.

Sadly, as a result of the CEOs' corrupt assault on Christian Values, that Organisation lost its financial accreditation, and had to suspend its operations.

Values are integral to our Identity. Values reveal our true Identity. If we are to be true to ourselves then we must behave in a way that is consistent with our Values. To claim to be Christian, but to live and act according to the Values of distorted Society, reveals our Hypocrisy.

This is not to imply that other Religions, and even pockets of secular Society, cannot also hold to worthy Values. I know such people who practice high moral Values, but do not claim to be Christian. But the cited Scriptures prove that these listed Values are part of the moral framework of true Christianity. Are Christians always perfect? No. But they aspire to these Values, because Jesus Himself demonstrated them. They want to become more and more like Jesus Christ!

This is the goal of every person who claims to be a CHRISTian: ***TO BECOME MORE AND MORE LIKE JESUS CHRIST.***

***

# Capsule 43 The Values Jesus Modelled And Promoted

See how Jesus modelled and promoted each of the Values listed in Capsule 42.

LOVE "While we were still sinners, Christ died for us" (Romans 5:8)

HOLINESS "God's holy servant Jesus" (Acts 4:27)

CHRISTLIKENESS "Love each other *as I have loved you*" (John 15:12)

INTEGRITY Jesus said "I am the Truth" (John 14:6)

TRANSPARENCY He challenged: "Can any of you prove me guilty?" John 8:46

JUSTICE "Christ suffered, the just for the unjust" 1 Peter 3:18

COMPETENCY "I have completed the work You gave me to do" (John 17:4)

SELF-SACRIFICE "Jesus Christ gave himself for our sins to rescue us" (Galatians 1:4)

CONTENTMENT Jesus did not complain that had no home (Luke 9:58)

FAITHFULNESS "Who can be trusted with little can be trusted with much" (Lk 16:10)

TEAMWORK "Jesus appointed 12 apostles to be with him .. to teach" (Mark 3:14)

ACCOUNTABILITY Jesus: "If you start working and look back, you are not fit" (Luke 9:62)

EXCELLENCE "God made the author of salvation (Jesus) perfect" (Hebrews 2:10)

SEXUAL PURITY "Anyone who looks lustfully .. commits adultery" (Matthew 5:28)

WORK "(Jesus) did not even have a chance to eat" (Mark 6:31)

HUMILITY Jesus "did not come to be served, but to serve" (Mark 10:45)

Jesus made disciples to follow Him, to become like Him in character and values.

As Jesus left this earth he told His disciples to go and make more disciples, who would follow Him and become like Him in character and values.

Those who don't, shame His reputation before the watching world.

Those who do, bring credit to the worthy reputation of Jesus.

# Part Thirteen

# Christians and Corruption

# Capsule 44 Is The Christian Church As Clean As It Claims To Be?

In fact, some claim that ONLY Christians can be morally good in society. Some years ago a Christian magazine quoted a certain Reverend as saying: "The church is the custodian, pillar and the upholder of truth, of ethics, of values, of Godliness and of holiness. These are characteristics *ONLY* found in the church" (emphasis mine).

Yet other news-items in the same magazine told another story:

- Bishops in the House of Lords are claiming up to £27,000 (around half-a-million Rand) a year in fixed-rate allowances, on top of their travel costs; some are claiming up to the maximum fixed allowance for attending sessions in the second chamber while having full-time jobs in their dioceses. Yet others attend sessions in the House without making any claim on the public purse.
- Members of various different religious groups who support gay marriage have launched a campaign against church leaders who have come out against same-sex marriage. Representatives from the Church of England, liberal Jews, the Quakers and the Unitarian and Free Church joined forces to declare their backing for the government's plans to legalise civil gay marriage, which have provoked strong opposition from leaders of the Anglican and Catholic churches

An editorial comment was perceptive: "It's getting harder to spot the difference between Hollywood producers and many professing evangelicals. One exalts self-interest, individualism, the acquisition of wealth and power at the expense of social responsibility, and doesn't care much about artistic integrity or excellence. And the other is a Hollywood producer."

***

# Capsule 45 Super-Efficiency In Spreading The Wrong Gospel

This is the headline of a 'Christianity Today' (16.2.2012) article that reports on the luxurious and expensive lifestyles of some Nigerian church leaders:

- A multi-million dollar private 10-seater jet with a range of 3900 nautical miles, given by his Word of Life Bible Church to Ayo Oritsejafor on the 40th anniversary of his ministry. He is President of the Christian Association of Nigeria.
- "Winners' Chapel" (Living Faith Ministries) founder, David Oyedepo, owns three Gulfstream jets, plus a Learjet, worth almost US$100 million.
- Other church leaders owning private jets are Enoch Adeboye, general overseer pf the Redeemed Christian Church of God; and Chris Oyakhilome, founder of Christ Embassy Church.

Apart from preachers, only top business tycoons and a few governors and politicians own private jets in a nation where more than 70 percent live on less than US$1 per day. Nigeria's wealthy have spent US$6.5 billion on private jets in the last five years, making it Africa's biggest market for private planes. The number of privately-owned aircraft rose by 650 percent between 2007 and 2012, up from 20 to 150 plancs at an average cost of US$50 million.

But most Christians in Africa's most-populous nation remain poor, fueling anger that these high-living pastors have been feeding fat on their parishioners.

Gideon Para Mallam, regional secretary of the International Fellowship of Evangelical Students, said such preachers are setting bad examples. "This represents another minus to Christianity in a country riddled with much corruption," he said. "We are simply displaying the rottenness of what has become of Nigeria. It is so sad."

Jeremiah Gado, president of the 3 million-strong Evangelical Church Winning All, agrees. "Having a private jet is a distraction and an indication of the lack of unity in the body."

But Oritsejafor defends the gift, maintaining that his private jet is a necessity and not a luxury. "Sometimes, my schedule is so complicated," he said at a press conference. "Now, I can move. I can even go and come back home. It is a bit more convenient for me", and I suspect that this is one of the reasons a lot of these other preachers have planes." Oritsefajor has his defenders. Wale Oke, national vice president, Pentecostal Fellowship of Nigeria (PFN) South West, sees a jet is just a tool for faster evangelization. He maintained Pentecostal preachers will buy more jets to cope with expanding ministries. "They ain't seen anything yet! More of us will yet buy and maintain our jets because, by the mercy of God, we have been given the wisdom to do so."

So we ask ourselves: Does "more convenient for me" justify this expensive extravagance?

What "message" is he preaching?

A "Gospel" of good news for the powerful church leaders, but not a Gospel for the common people.

A "Gospel of Prosperity", not the "Gospel of Jesus Christ who, though he was rich, became poor"

A "Gospel of Materialism" which is more important than the spiritual wealth which Jesus came to give us, in which compassion, love, sharing are key components.

This Gospel that is being spread faster by the super-wealthy is not the Gospel of Jesus! His Gospel calls us to *"Come follow me - deny yourself and take up the cross daily"*. The Prosperity Gospel cannot warn people that *"there is no profit in gaining the world when you lose your own souls".* (Luke 9:23-25).

These preachers are super-efficient in spreading the *wrong gospel.*

***

# Capsule 46 Church Salary Comparisons: North America 2016

Ponder this excerpt from Warren Bird's 2016 Salary analysis, USA

(downloaded 25.7.2017; Rand equivalents as in 2017)

1. **Do staff-heavy churches pay the same as their same-size counterparts with fewer paid staff?**

Actually, they pay more. Suppose you compare churches in the bottom 20% of the attender-to-staff ratios ("staff heavy") with similar-size churches in the top 20% of the attender-to-staff ratios ("lean staff"). If a senior pastor in the staff-heavy group makes $177,000 annually *(= R2 301 000 pa =R191750 pm)*, the counterpart in the lean-staff church makes $156,000 *(=R2 028 000 pa = R169 000pm)*. Likewise looking at *averages for the entire senior staff*, if the median in the staff-heavy church is $70,000 *(=R75 833pm)*, the median in the lean-staff church is $60,000. *(=R65 000 pm)*

## 2. Custom Compensation and Benefit Analysis:

Our partner Vanderbloemen Search Group, a premier church consulting firm, provides a tailored, objective compensation analysis specifically geared to your church's size, geographic setting, specific job descriptions, and type of church.

Dave Travis, CEO of Leadership Network advises, "Every church with income over 2 million dollars *(= R26 million)* needs a custom survey every two or three years because:

- It mitigates the legal risk of your church regarding compensation. An analysis can help avoid potential blindspots for churches regarding pay, severance, and benefits.

- The competition for quality staff is high and you never want people to leave because their compensation package.
- You never want to be surprised with "sticker shock" when you go to hire a new position. You might as well *be competitive at all times*.
- Scrutiny is constantly increasing on these issues from outside groups and governmental agencies. The wise approach is to have outside help give you qualified opinions to help you make well-informed choices."

This survey indicates how 'worldly' the church has become. The Church, especially in affluent countries, is becoming "conformed to this world", with remuneration packages in competition with each other. Materialism is a major factor in USA, and it is spilling over into South Africa too. Pastors want ever higher salaries. They compare with higher executive salaries in the business world.

Does it matter if "outside groups and governmental agencies" are scrutinising the Church by their materialistic standards? Where are the uniquely Christian Values? Where is the sacrificial dedication of yesteryear?

Yes, it does matter. The Church of Jesus should not be accountable to, or measured by, the standards of the world. It should be accountable to its Master, Jesus Christ. He has given us His standards in Scripture. Judge the Church - yes, but judge it by Jesus' criteria. Then the watching world will not be able to validly condemn the Church for its behaviour, for if they do, they will be condemning Jesus and His criteria.

\*\*\*

# Capsule 47 Famous Pastor Convicted Of Embezzling Church Funds

[Originally published in The Christian Post. Source: Gateway News 28.2.2014}

The pastor of Yoido Full Gospel Church in Seoul, South Korea, Yonggi Cho, was convicted last week of embezzling $12 million of the church's funds. His church grew to become famous as the largest congregation in the world. I visited his church in 1993. On a Sunday, he led 10 successive services. As one service ended, the people left by doors on one side, while others filed in through doors on the other side. This church had 5000 satellite congregations, linked to the central church by satellite TV. Cho had a huge following.

But at the age of 78, Cho was sentenced to three years in prison after he was convicted of directing officials to buy stocks from his son at four times the market price. The church subsequently lost U.S. $12 million, according to The Gospel Herald. Hee-jun, Cho's oldest son, the former CEO of the media company, Kookmin Ilbo, was also sentenced last week to three years in prison for his participation in the embezzlement scheme.

However, American megachurch pastor, Bob Rodgers defends Cho, whom he refers to as "a personal friend of the family". He and his father had served on Cho's church board for a combined 38 years.

According to Rodgers, Cho did not purposely sabotage his church, but rather, his son "purposely defrauded" him. "Cho testified that he trusted his elders and son and didn't check and read the thousands of pages of paperwork, which was prepared for him to sign. Because Cho relied upon the direction of his choice elders and son, he signed the papers. He never received any monies from the transaction," Rodgers wrote. In fact Cho lived in a modest 1000 sq ft church apartment, and does not own a car. Cho has raised and given personally to the church more than $170 million," he wrote.

Rodgers added that Cho is likely to avoid prison time but instead be placed on probation.

However, Rodger's interpretation of Cho's trial contrasts with the account of former elder, Ha Sang-ok. In November Ha said that he had attempted unsuccessfully to convince the pastor to end his unethical ways.

"A sect leader might violate the commandments and do as he wishes, but a pastor cannot do that," He said, as reported in *The Hanyoreah*. "Over the past 14 years, I have met with Rev. Cho many times to try to persuade him to repent and return to being a great pastor, but the corruption has continued. That's why I had no choice but to disclose it to the outside world."

South Korea's Courts weighed the evidence and pronounced their 'guilty' verdict.

As I read this sad report, my first reaction was "There, but for the grace of God, go I" James 3:1 sounds this warning: *"Not many of you should presume to be teachers, my brothers, because we know that we who teach will be judged more strictly"*. Few people can handle such immense power and influence well. Rather plant 5000 small 'independent' churches than lead ONE church with 5000 satellite churches. I'm nervous about the trend to mega-churches and multi-site churches, under the leadership of powerful mega-pastors.

Expansive power invites temptations.

When a Christian leader begins to sense that too much power is accruing to him, when his church is becoming a mega-church with a growing staff, when his budget is becoming larger than average, then it is time to seriously 'decentralise the power'. Encourage some of his members to plant a new church elsewhere, call their own pastor and so expand the influence of Jesus and His Kingdom as a local church in its own right. Such a strategy wisely recognises the danger of too much power. Power corrupts, and total power corrupts totally. New Testament believers would meet in house-churches as well as in larger venues. (Acts 2:46, Rom ans 16:5, 1Corinthians 16:19)

# Part Fourteen

# The Power of Example

# *Capsule 48* Integrity Is Expressed By Principled Behaviour

When reading Integrity Capsules on the pages of this book, it is easy to mentally endorse the principles of Integrity. One could study it, and pass an examination on it. One could readily claim to be FOR Integrity and AGAINST Fraud and Corruption.

Ask any leader, corporate executive or politician "Are you in favour of Corruption?" and the answer will always be "NO! of course not." It is not politically correct to endorse Corruption. After all, it is a crime. And who would self-incriminate her/himself? Everybody wants to be known as having Integrity, and opposing Corruption.

That is why, in the final analysis, Integrity is demonstrated by BEHAVIOUR. By what one does - not by what one says. And this cuts both ways:

If you live an exemplary life of Integrity, you set an example that influences others to choose a lifestyle of Integrity. That is why **PART FIFTEEN will tell Good Stories that demonstrate Integrity.** These encourage us to follow their example.

Principled Behaviour is costly. Whoever chooses to behave with principled ethics soon find s/he is swimming against the tide. Others feel threatened by a person of Integrity. Read again the dangerous story of ex-ANC MP Makhosi Khoza as told in Capsule 51.

She followed her conscience which prioritised the Principles of Integrity, and this led her to resign from the ANC, her political home for 35 years. She was ridiculed by her former colleagues, she and her family received threats. This was the price she paid for Integrity.

Her example lives on. Those who value Integrity admire her.

Her Integrity is not only expressed by her words. It is most clearly seen in her behaviour. She did not only say she was against corruption

- she demonstrated it by her courageous protest, and then by her resignation from the Party that was associated with corruption.

***

# Capsule 49 The Bad Example of Leaders Who Reject Integrity

### To Do Their Own Thing

Many other witnesses before the Commission on State Capture have reported similar experiences. In a number of testimonies, ex President Jacob Zuma has been accused of capturing the State for his own benefit.

Commissioner Deputy Chief Justice Raymond Zondo, wanting to give Zuma a fair and just opportunity to defend himself, subpoenaed him to appear before the Commission to give his side of the story. He refused to answer questions, saying that he didn't want to incriminate himself. The ex-President then demanded that Zondo recuse himself, because Zuma alleged he was biased against him. The Commissioner refused. So Zuma walked out, without permission to leave - an illegal action. Zondo then appealed to the highest Court in the land, the Constitutional Court, which ordered Zuma to appear before the Commission as scheduled on 15<sup>th</sup> February 2021. Zuma then defied the ConCourt, announcing he would not come as required.

Unsurprisingly for most people, the Secretary-General of the ANC, Ace Magashule (who himself is out on bail in another Corruption case), openly supported Zuma's decision. In response to reporters' questions, he said:

> "Let's leave President Zuma alone. What is the problem? What has Zuma done? President Zuma is a South African. He has his own rights, so you can't ask me to talk on behalf of President Zuma... President Zuma has a right to do whatever he wants to do."

Here is the worst of all examples to follow. Yet Ace makes the ANC's position clear:

"Zuma has the right to do whatever he wants to do." But look at the background ...

- Zuma has twice publicly taken an Oath to uphold the Constitution.
- When he was President, in 2017, Zuma himself appointed the State Capture Commission.
- He appointed Deputy Chief Justice Raymond Zondo as the Commissioner.
- At that time, Zuma urged everyone to respect the Commission and obey its decress.

Now, because he "has the right to do whatever he wants to do", he has the right to break his Oath and to despise the State Capture Commission which he had appointed. He has the right to disobey his own instruction to respect and obey the Commission.

*If this example is followed by the nation,*
*everyone will "do whatever they want to do".*
*The Rule of Law will cease to exist.*
*Anarchy will prevail. South Africa will crash.*

Many will eagerly follow Zuma's example and defy the Law. Many will embrace Magashule's reasoning, and "do whatever they want to do." Already, for some years, the laws have been flouted:

!!! See how the kombi-taxis break every traffic rule with impunity.

!!! See the growing incidents of Gender-based Violence, in spite of repeated pleas to cease this brutal practice.

!!! See the many who flout that Protocols necessary to curb the spread of COVID-19.

!!! See how ESKOM's frequent load-shedding was caused in large part by illegal electricity connections, and by refusal to pay for electricity.

!!! See how much money is lost to those who make money by illegally stealing cables.

Too often there are no consequences for these illegal activities.
*(source: IOL reporter 3.2.2021, headlined "Defending Zuma's lack of Integrity".)*

The scary power of a Bad Example!

# Part Fifteen

# Good Stories

# *Capsule 50* Billy Graham Protects His Team with Integrity

This world-renowned Christian leader and confidant of some USA Presidents, Billy preached Christ personally to more than 218 million people face to face in 185 countries. He left his mark as a man of Integrity. When he died in 2018, at the age of 98, a TV documentary themed its record under the title of "Integrity". Unlike some international Christian TV personalities, he had no scandals to his name. He had stood humbly strong against the temptations that come through Fame and Power. He credited God for this.

Billy Graham was great in personal integrity. When asked in the sunset years of his ministry what he would like to be remembered for, he would often say, "Integrity. I want to be remembered for having integrity." One of the crowning achievements of his ministry has been his scandal free ministerial career both morally, and financially.

Billy Graham's inspiring example of moral and financial integrity exhibited in his **Modesto Manifesto** was a breath of fresh air in the midst of many well-publicized failures of other evangelical leaders.

**"One afternoon during the meetings in Modesto, I asked the Team to go to their rooms for an hour and list all the problems they could think of that evangelists and evangelism encountered.**

**When they returned, the lists were remarkably similar, and in a short amount of time, we made a series of resolutions or commitments among ourselves that would guide us in our future evangelistic work. In reality, it was more of an informal understanding among ourselves - a shared commitment to do all we could do to uphold**

the Bible's standard of absolute integrity and purity for evangelists.

The first point on our combined list was money. Nearly all evangelists at that time - including us - were supported by love offerings taken at the meetings. The temptation to wring as much money as possible out of an audience, often with strong emotional appeals, was too great for some evangelists. In addition, there was little or no accountability for finances. It was a system that was easy to abuse—and led to the charge that evangelists were in it only for the money.

I had been drawing a salary from YFC (Youth for Christ) and turning all offerings from YFC meetings over to YFC committees, but my new independent efforts in citywide campaigns required separate finances. In Modesto we determined to do all we could to avoid financial abuses and to downplay the offering and depend as much as possible on money raised by the local committee in advance.

The second item on the list was the danger of sexual immorality. We all knew of evangelists who had fallen into immorality while separated from their families by travel. We pledged among ourselves to avoid any situation that would have even the appearance of compromise or suspicion. From that day on, I did not travel, meet or eat alone with a woman other than my wife. We determined that the Apostle Paul's mandate to the young pastor Timothy would be ours as well: *"Flee ... youthful lusts"* (2 Timothy 1:22, KJV).

Our third concern was the tendency of many evangelists to work apart from the local church, even to criticize local pastors and churches openly and scathingly. We were convinced, however, that this was not only counterproductive but also wrong from the Bible's standpoint. We determined to cooperate with all who would cooperate with us in the public proclamation of the Gospel, and to avoid an antichurch or anti-clergy attitude.

The fourth and final issue was publicity. The tendency among some evangelists was to exaggerate their successes or to claim higher attendance numbers than they really had. This likewise discredited evangelism and brought the whole enterprise under suspicion. It often made the press so suspicious of evangelists that they refused to take notice of their work. In Modesto we committed ourselves to integrity in our publicity and our reporting."

So much for the Modesto Manifesto, as Cliff (Barrows) called it in later years. In reality, it did not mark a radical departure for us; we had always held these principles. It did, however, settle in our hearts and minds, once and for all, the determination that integrity would be the hallmark of both our lives and our ministry. Cliff added: "Billy Graham's commitment to integrity stems from his relationship with Christ. You can know Christ, too".

\*\*\*

# Capsule 51 Makhosi Khoza - Suffering For Integrity Of Conscience

Khoza became involved with the ANC in the early 1980s, aged 12, and became a Member of Parliament in 2014. Dr Makhosi would later table her membership resignation from ANC, citing her renewed dedication to combat and eradicate corruption.

Dr Makhosi Khoza is a competent political figure and an anti-corruption vocalist in South Africa. She is better known for her lead runner roles in Jacob Zuma's removal from office. Besides her vocal political career, Dr Makhosi is a caring mother to her two children. Her firm stand and accomplishments sufficiently justify her clean legislative record.

In 2021, at the Zondo Commission former ANC MP Makhosi Khoza testified that "Anyone who tried to protect the rule of law in the (ruling Party the) African National Congress would be punished." She set out how she became disillusioned with the leadership of former president Jacob Zuma, and how her party set out to silence her often critical voice.

Minister Faith Muthambi told Khoza that former president Jacob Zuma would consider her for finance minister if she accepted only "one boss" – Zuma himself. Loyalty to the ANC and its leader was more important than her conscience. This is seen in this story:

Initially, she served on the Standing Committee on Finance (SCOF). She recalled a SCOF meeting, where board chairperson of the South African Airways, Dudu Myeni, outlined a plan to fire old, white pilots and replace them with young, black pilots. Khoza questioned Myeni's plan, saying that the SAA is lauded for its safety record, thanks to those pilots. In a heated debate, her ANC colleagues said she is anti-transformation.

**Khoza said she understands transformation, not only in terms of pigmentation, but also in terms of the integrity of systems, but that it also requires competency.**

Van Rooyen (notorious for his brief tenure as an incompetent Minister of Finance) told her she was "counter-revolutionary" and asked why she had questioned "Comrade Dudu". She was told to never question comrades.

Khoza was also selected to serve on the ad hoc committee, which investigated the South African Broadcasting Corporation board. A scholar and scientist herself, Khoza was not impressed by the appointment of the unqualified Hlaudi Motsoeneng as SABC COO, who had a raft of Public Protector findings against him. Muthambi later told Khoza, on the sidelines of the ad hoc committee, that if her "one boss" Zuma was happy with Motsoeneng's qualifications, then she was too.

Khoza said the late Jackson Mthembu's predecessor as ANC chief whip, Stone Sizani, didn't appreciate parliamentary oversight over the executive. He never took it kindly when we criticised the executive as members of the ANC.

After she saw the public protest against Zuma, when he fired Pravin Gordhan as finance minister in April 2017, she began to publicly express her criticism of the party leadership. When they received orders that they were to protect Zuma at all costs "I then decided to defy the leadership," she said. "They wanted us to protect something that was wrong." She was called ill-disciplined. and she said Mthembu grew "increasingly uncomfortable" with her. "He didn't take kindly to me criticising the ANC."

The secretariat, Mantashe and Duarte, told the caucus the ANC was under attack, and they needed to defend the party. Mantashe said an attack on the ANC's president is an attack on the whole organisation.

Khoza said she didn't agree: It was one man, Zuma, who was a liability for the ANC. Mantashe said voting with the opposition in a motion of no confidence in Zuma would be the highest form of betrayal.

At the ANC policy conference in July 2017, Fikile Mbalula, currently transport minister, threatened MPs who wanted to vote according to their conscience, likening them to suicide bombers. Khoza received various threats, and these included some to her family.

For the most part, she delivered her testimony matter-of-factly, but a hint of emotion entered her voice when she spoke of the threats to her family. She lost her husband when she was 28 and her son was one year old.

People came to her house and told her son that she killed her husband. "I now had to start defending myself. They were making my life at home miserable," she said. She said her academic work was also scuppered because of her dissident stance.

Khoza recalled an incident, where she spotted a black Mercedes Benz in her neighbour's driveway upon her arrival home. A person, clad in a black balaclava and gloves, slipped as he took his shot at her. "That's how I survived." She said there were several other threats as well. "My children were forever worried whether I would come back alive."

She pointed out that she lives in KwaZulu-Natal, a province known for its political violence.

Khoza was one of the ANC MPs who voted in support of a motion of no confidence in Zuma in August 2017, and she made her vote known. She said, on 14 August 2017, that Zuma had said the ANC's unity is paramount, and that steps should be taken against those MPs who voted with their conscience. The following day, Mantashe announced that the ANC's national working committee had decided to institute disciplinary steps against the four MPs who voted with their conscience.

The Commission Chair, Deputy Chief Justice Raymond Zondo, asked if she understood this to mean that they were expected to ignore the ruling by the Constitutional Court. Khoza answered in the affirmative. Zondo said: 'It is bad enough when it is said by any party, but when it is said by the ruling party, it is even worse, it seems to me. I can't understand that. I can't understand how that could be."

In response, Khoza said: "The situation in the ANC was that anyone who sought to uphold the rule of law would be punished. I'm a living example of this."

Khoza left the ANC – and, after stints at the African Democratic Change Party and OUTA, she is now with Herman Mashaba's fledgling ActionSA Party.

Her story shows how, in political culture, 'Loyalty to the ANC' is more important than the Integrity of one's Conscience. She was prepared to suffer, and she did, for prioritising Integrity over blind Loyalty to the ANC. What a glowing example for others to note and follow!

\*\*\*

# Capsule 52 Imtiaz Sooliman - Gift Of the Givers "An Angel Among Men"

## Contentment Displaces Materialism, Inhibits Corruption

(702's Money Show - Every Monday Bruce Whitfield interviews famous people about their attitude to Money. On 4 July 2019 he interviewed Dr Imtiaz Sooliman)

"I have no desire for clothes. I have no desire for holidays. I have no desire for outings. All I see is the suffering of people... I have no pension plan, because I don't have much earnings... My father told me I'm crazy... He's passed on now, but several years ago he told me 'I'm proud of you'..."

Dr Imtiaz Sooliman is the Founder and Director of "Gift of the Givers", an international charity, based in South Africa. He studied for years to become a medical doctor. He never planned it, but in 1992 he left his previous life behind forever, and created "Gift of the Givers". Since then his organisation has traveled to the world's most horrific places, helping millions.

"I'm a very simple person. I don't have any materialistic thoughts or desires. I had a good practice. I changed cars six times in five years. I travelled overseas. Nothing of those kinds of things interest me anymore. I have no desire for clothes. I have no desire for holidays. I have no desire for outings. Because all I see is the suffering of people..."

(We note that when one is focused on "the suffering of other people", then selfish desires fade. And when selfish desires fade, then Greed dissolves, and the temptation to Fraud and Corruption disappear. Dr Sooliman has highlighted the answer to the plague of Corruption - 'Contentment', the lack of materialistic desires.)

"On 6 August 1992 when I was 28 years old – it was a Thursday night – I was in Istanbul with a spiritual teacher. There were people from all countries, all religions, and all colours – there was a unity of man, of different groupings in a holy place. After a religious ceremony the teacher just looked at me and it was as if something was talking through him – he just looked at me and said:

'My son I'm not asking you. I'm instructing you. You will form an organisation; the name will be Gift of the Givers. You will serve all people of all races, of all religions, of allcolours, of all classes, of all political affiliations and of any geographical location and you will serve them unconditionally. You will not expect anything in return - not even a thank you. In fact, with the kind of duty that you're going to do, expect to get kicked in the butt. If you don't get kicked regard that as a bonus. Serve the people with kindness, with compassion, with mercy and remember the dignity of man is foremost – no matter what condition there is, you always protect the dignity of man and, when you serve them, serve them with excellence. This is an instruction for you for the rest of your life. Remember that whatever is done is done *through* you and not *by* you. Don't ever forget that!'

Dr Imtiaz Sooliman, described the attitude of Gift of the Givers to money: "Nobody works here for the money. Their only aim is to help people in need." When asked who donated R2.3 billion in funding for Gift of the Givers? He answered: "South Africans!"

"We don't have international funders! 99.9% of the money is from ordinary South Africans... South Africa is one of the most generous nations on Earth... People still dig into their pockets... Even for international projects... In 2011 when we responded to the famine in Somalia... a poor school in Orange Farm – the kids don't have shoes, they don't have lunch, they don't have a jersey in winter – gave us R41 000... When parents pray for their children, those prayers are answered."

Money is important... you need a certain amount... [But] What you don't use is not yours... You can only drive one car at a time, and you can only sleep in one bed at a time. I hope everybody makes a lot of money...

it's very good! I pray as many people as possible have the means to not depend on anybody.

When asked what scares him about money, he replied "Greed and extravagance and power."

As we have seen earlier, GREED and POWER are driving forces in CORRUPTION. In Dr Sooliman's view, these are dangerous temptations which must be avoided. We must use money, Money must never use us. It is not Money itself, but *"the LOVE of Money* that *is the root of all evil."* (1 Timothy 6:10).

# Part Sixteen

# Conclusion

# Capsule 53 Into The Future With Integrity

Congratulations! You have swallowed 52 capsules in this Immunisation Program!

Have you digested them?

As we sampled instances that describe the Face of Corruption in its many expressions, we gained an insight into the scourge that is dragging our nation into moral and economic misery.

Greed is the INSIDE story of Corruption. Each of us recognises that it's not only others, but *"I am by nature a Greedy person"* and subject to the temptation to Corruption. The antidote is CONTENTMENT.

From the Capsules that I have swallowed and digested, I will reject material Greed as a habit.

Instead I will consciously embrace CONTENTMENT as a habitual way of life.

With this conscious COMMITMENT to CONTENTMENT I will move forward into a new Chapter of my life. And if I slip and fall, I will get up again and continue my upward climb.

**Signed** _____ **on** **Date**

_____

**NOW**

What about the OUTSIDE story of Corruption? The many OPPORTUNITIES to be corrupt?

I will urge others to join me in WHISTLE-BLOWING, reporting on all the Corruption we notice.

Re-read Capsule 11, on the steps we can take to report Fraud and Corruption.

https://www.corruptionwatch.org.za
report@corruptionwatch.org.za
https://accountabilitynow.org.za


**And We Can Even Go Further**

Lobby the Department of Justice to tighten up their response to Fraud and Corruption. The current response is tame, quite out of proportion to the damage caused.

The offender is punished by a term of imprisonment. Each inmate costs taxpayer R9,876.35 per month - Sbu Ndebele. That means you pay R11 851.62 for each year s/he is in prison.

**https://www.politicsweb.co.za/documents/each-inmate-costs-taxpayer-r987635-per-month—sbu-**[1]

Add this to the amount of money which has already been stolen through corruption. The cost is huge! Corruption costs the SA gross domestic product (GDP) at least R27 billion annually- as well as the loss of 76 000 jobs that would otherwise have been created, according to Minister of Economic Development Ebrahim Patel.

**www.businesstech.co.za/news/government/196116/corruption-costs-sa-gdp-at-least-r27-billion-annually-and-76-000-jo bs/**[2]

Surely Justice cannot close its eyes to this Injustice! Why drain the fiscus further by providing free board and lodging to those who have already cost the tax-payers so much?

---

1.    https://www.politicsweb.co.za/documents/each-inmate-costs-taxpayer-r987635-per-month--sbu-

2.    http://www.businesstech.co.za/news/government/196116/corruption-costs-sa-gdp-at-least-r27-billion-annually-and-76-000-jo%20bs/

This is where South Africa could find its direction from African Traditional Customary Law. This does not see "imprisonment" as the appropriate Consequence for wrong-doing. Rather, it provides for RESTITUTION. If my cattle destroy my neighbour's crops, the tribal council requires me to pay my neighbour for the value of the crops destroyed. If my son impregnates a girl, I must pay a fine to the girl's father. For Africans, RESTITUTION is the suitable Consequence of the crime.

RESTITUTION happens to be the Biblical Consequence as well. Exodus chapters 21 and 22 list Case-Law examples covering a wide range of crimes, as well as accidental damages. The RESTITUTION for 'Theft' is higher: twice, four of five times the value of the stolen property (Exodus 22:1,7,9). When the tax-collector Zacchaeus had his life-changing encounter with Jesus, he of his own accord promised to pay back four times the amount he had gained by cheating (Luke 19:8). Today's Fraud and Corruption would fall under this "theft" category.

Would not RESTITUTION, instead of Imprisonment, be a much fairer Consequence for those convicted of Fraud and Corruption? It would also be a stronger deterrent, because it would cancel out the gains of Greed - the culprit would be hit in the pocket where it hurts most. And everyone would readily agree that this was a Just Consequence.

Lobby the Department of Justice to tighten up their response to Fraud and Corruption. Argue the case for the African Justice Value of RESTITUTION. The current response is tame, quite out of proportion to the damage caused. In fact, Imprisonment compounds the costly damage of the corruption itself.

**https://www.justice.gov.za/contact/contact_list.html**
Email: **CPhiri@justice.gov.za**

**May each reader have the moral courage
to live a life-style of Integrity,**

to avoid every hint of Corruption, and to report all instances of
Corruption, without fear or favour.

Then to encourage others to do the same.

Capsules provided by
Hugh G Wetmore
Tel 012 3482913 Cell 072 2524789
Email: wetmore@singingtheword.co.za

# Appendices

Express your Commitment to INTEGRITY
with the help of these sample Codes of Integrity and Ethics
for PERSONAL, CORPORATE, GOVERNMENT and
CHRISTIAN SERVICE Contexts

# Appendix 1 Code for Personal Integrity

**The Unashamedly Ethical**
**revised Personal Commitment certificate 11.11.2014**

To be entirely truthful in all I say.

To be faithful to my family relationships.

To do nothing out of selfish ambition or conceit, but to look out for the interests of others.

To refuse to elicit, accept or pay any bribes and to encourage others to do the same.

To be diligent without being harsh, and striving to be just and fair.

To be a peacemaker.

To do my work wholeheartedly.

To submit myself to just and ethical governing authorities.

To remember the poor by investing generously and sacrificially in the broader community.

To collaborate with my peers to impact our community and nation.

# Appendix 2 Code for Corporate Integrity

**The SGS Code of Integrity**

**SGS** is the world's leading inspection, verification, testing and certification company. We are recognized as the global benchmark for quality and integrity. With more than 89,000 employees, we operate a network of more than 2,600 offices and laboratories around the world.

This is one of the most comprehensive Codes of Integrity or Ethics I have seen. I recommend it for study (and considered emulation) by those in the corporate world. Read the full document on this link:

**https://www.sgs.co.za/-/media/global/documents/ brochures/code-of-integrity/sgs-compliance-code-of-integrity-a4-english-uk.pdf**

Here is a brief excerpt relating to SGS' **Principles of Integrity**:

- **"Trust:** this is our single most valuable asset, the foundation of our brand and reputation. Customers rely on our integrity and this trust needs to be nurtured and safeguarded day after day. It can be jeopardised in an instant.
- **Honesty and transparency:** in everything that we do, we need to be truthful to ourselves, our customers and colleagues. No circumstances justify lies, deceit or a lack of honesty.
- **Accountability:** each of our actions and omissions has consequences. We accept the consequences of our choices and do not blame others for our actions.
- **Ethical Principles:** we believe in acting ethically, in fairness and respect for others. Our decisions will be guided by respect for principles and standards of good behaviour, not by arbitrary choices or personal preferences."

## ASK YOURSELF THE RIGHT QUESTIONS

- Do I suspect that the particular course of action may be illegal or unethical?
- How would this look if this decision were reported in a newspaper, or if I were to talk about this with my family and friends?
- Does the proposed course of action involve lying or being untruthful?
- Could the proposed course of action endanger the personal safety or health of others?
- Could the proposed course of action damage SGS or its reputation?
- Does the transaction have a legitimate business purpose?

If the proposed course of action fails any of these tests, you should seek advice and re-consider your decision."

# Appendix 3 Code for Government Integrity

## CODE OF ETHICS AND BUSINESS CONDUCT FOR THE GAUTENG PROVINCIAL GOVERNMENT

### Gauteng Shared Service Centre

### I INTRODUCTION

This document comprises the Code of Ethics and Business Conduct for the Gauteng Provincial Government.

Why should there be a Code of Ethics and Business Conduct? The purpose of such a Code is the following:

- To serve as a brief description of the Gauteng Provincial Government's core values;
- To provide a framework for identifying conduct that is ethical and acceptable for the employees and officials of the Gauteng Provincial Government who, effectively, act as its agents at all levels;
- To create the context for the ethical use of authority; and
- To support all efforts aimed at curbing moral degeneration.

### II SCOPE OF THIS CODE

1. This Code of Ethics and Business Conduct applies to the following persons:

a) All officials/employees of the Gauteng Provincial Government.

## III ETHICS

Why should there be standards of ethics?

- To ensure that all stakeholders within the Gauteng Provincial Government are aware of the basic values cherished by the Gauteng Provincial Government, its employees (including management) and officials; and
- To ensure accountability within the Gauteng Provincial Government in terms of fundamental ethical values and value systems.

What are the fundamental ethical standards cherished and expected by the Gauteng Provincial Government?

The Gauteng Provincial Government cherishes the following values and ideals:

- Absolute integrity;
- A culture of honesty;
- Loyalty;
- Professionalism;
- Acceptance of responsibility and accountability;
- A positive public image;
- Confidence from the public;
- Striving for and maintaining credibility;
- High standards of service delivery;
- A sense of pride in belonging to the Department;
- Sanctioning (punishing - ed.) bad, and rewarding good behavior; and
- All other positive attributes contributing toward sound ethical standards.

## IV THE CODE OF CONDUCT

The Gauteng Provincial Government subscribes wholly to the Code of Conduct for the Public Service as detailed in the Public Service Regulations and which is reflected verbatim below.

## *"CODE OF CONDUCT FOR THE PUBLIC SERVICE*
## *A. PURPOSE*

A.1 In order to give practical effect to the relevant constitutional provisions relating to the public service, all employees are expected to comply with the Code of Conduct provided for in this Chapter.

A.2 The Code should act as a guideline to employees as to what is expected of them from an ethical point of view, both in their individual conduct and in their relationship with other. Compliance with the Code can be expected to enhance professionalism and help to ensure confidence in the public service.

## *B. INTRODUCTION:*

B.1 The need exists to provide direction to employees with regard to their relationship with the legislature, political and executive office-bearers, other employees and the public and to indicate the spirit in which employees should perform their duties, what should be done to avoid conflicts of interests and what is expected of them in terms of their personal conduct in public and private life.

B.2 Although the code of Conduct was drafted to be as comprehensive as possible, it is not an exhaustive set of rules regulating standards of conduct. However, heads of department, by virtue of their responsibility in terms of section 7 (3) (b) of the Act for the efficient management and administration of their departments and the maintenance of discipline, are, inter alia, under a duty to ensure that the conduct of their employees conforms to the basic values and principles governing public administration and the norms and standards prescribed by the Act. Heads of department should also ensure that their staff are acquainted with these measures, and that they accept and abide by them.

B.3 The primary purpose of the Code is a positive one, viz. to promote exemplary conduct. Notwithstanding this, an employee shall be guilty of misconduct, and may be dealt with in accordance with the relevant collective agreement if she or he contravenes any provision of the Code of Conduct or fails to comply with any provision thereof.

## C. CODE OF CONDUCT
## C.1 RELATIONSHIP WITH THE LEGISLATURE AND THE EXECUTIVE An employee –

C.1.1 is faithful to the Republic and honors the Constitution and abides thereby in the execution of her or his daily tasks;

C.1.2 puts the public interest first in the execution of her or his duties;

C.1.3 loyally executes the policies of the Government of the day in the performance of her or his official duties as contained in all statutory and other prescripts;

C.1.4 strives to be familiar with and abides by all statutory and other instructions applicable to her or his conduct and duties; and

C.1.5 co-operates with public institutions established under legislation and the Constitution in promoting the public interest.

## C.2 RELATIONSHIP WITH THE PUBLIC
An employee –

C.2.1 promotes the unity and well-being of the South African nation in performing her or his official duties;

C.2.2 will serve the public in an unbiased and impartial manner in order to create confidence in the public service;

C.2.3 is polite, helpful and reasonably accessible in her or his dealing with the public, at all times treating members of the public as customers who are entitled to receive high standards of service;

C.2.4 has regard for the circumstances and concerns of the public in performing her or his official duties and in the making of decisions affecting them;

C.2.5 is committed through timely service to the development and upliftment of all South Africans;

C.2.6 does not unfairly discriminate against any member of the public on account of race, gender, ethnic or social origin, color, sexual orientation, age, disability, religion, political persuasion, conscience, belief, culture or language;

C.2.7 does not abuse her or his position in the public service to promote or prejudice the interest of any political party or interest group;

C.2.8 respects and protects every person's dignity and her or his rights as contained in the Constitution; and

C.2.9 recognizes the public's right of access to information, excluding information that is specifically protected by law.

## C.3 RELATIONSHIPS AMONG EMPLOYEES
An employee –
C.3.1 co-operates fully with other employees to advance the public interest;

C.3.2 executes all reasonable instructions by persons officially assigned to give them, provided these are not contrary to the provisions of the Constitution and/or any other law;

C.3.3 refrains from favouring relatives and friends in work-related activities and never abuses her or his authority or influences other employee, nor is influenced to abuse her or his authority;

C.3.4 uses the appropriate channels to air her or his grievances or to direct representations; C.3.5 is committed to the optimal development, motivation and utilisation of her or his staff

and the promotion of sound labour and interpersonal relations;C.3.6 deals fairly, professionally and equitably with other employees, irrespective of race, gender, ethnic or social origin, colour, sexual orientation, age, disability, religion, political persuasion, conscience, belief, culture or language; and

C.3.7 refrains from party political activities in the workplace.
## C.4 PERFORMANCE OF DUTIES

An employee –

C.4.1 strives to achieve the objectives of her or his institution cost-effectively and in the public's interest;

C.4.2 is creative in thought and in the execution of her or his duties, seeks innovative ways to solve problems and enhances effectiveness and efficiency within the context of the law;

C.4.3 is punctual in the execution of her or his duties;

C.4.4 executes her or his duties in a professional and competent manner;

C.4.5 does not engage in any transaction or action that is in conflict with or infringes on the execution of her or his official duties;

C.4.6 will recuse herself or himself from any official action or decision-making process which may result in improper personal gain, and this should be properly declared by the employee;

C.4.7 accepts the responsibility to avail herself or himself of ongoing training and self-development throughout her or his career;

C.4.8 is honest and accountable in dealing with public funds and uses the public service's property and other resources effectively, efficiently, and only for authorised official purposes;

C.4.9 promotes sound, efficient, effective, transparent and accountable administration; C.4.10 in the course of her or his official duties, shall report to the appropriate authorities,

> fraud, corruption, nepotism, maladministration and any other act which constitutes an offence, or which is prejudicial to the public interest;

> C.4.11 gives honest and impartial advice, based on all available relevant information, to higher authority when asked for assistance of this kind; and

> C.4.12 honors the confidentiality of matters, documents and discussions,classified or implied as being confidential or secret.

## C.5 PERSONAL CONDUCT AND PRIVATE INTERESTS
An employee –

C.5.1 during official duties, dresses and behaves in a manner that enhances thereputation of the public service;

C.5.2 acts responsibly as far as the use of alcoholic beverages or any othersubstance with an intoxicating effect is concerned;

C.5.3 does not use her or his official position to obtain private gifts or benefitsfor herself or himself during the performance of her or his official duties nor does she or he accept any gifts or benefits when offered as these may be construed as bribes;

C.5.4 does not use or disclose any official information for personal gain or the gain of others; and

C.5.5 does not, without approval, undertake remunerative work outside her orhis official duties or use office equipment for such work."

## V QUESTIONABLE SITUATIONS

An employee or official, who has doubts regarding a questionable situation that might arise, should immediately consult her or his Manager who will secure clarity from the Director for Human Resource Management.

VI APPROVAL (Signed)"

(http://www.dpsa.gov.za/dpsa2g/documents/accc/ Public%20Service%20Code%20of%20Conduct.pdf)

# Appendix 4 Code for Integrity in Christian Ministry

**The National Association of Evangelicals (in the USA)**
**Code of Ethics for the Christian Ministry**

*Whatever happens, conduct yourselves in a manner worthy of the gospel of Christ. (Philippians 1:27)*

*We put no stumbling block in anyone's path, so that our ministry will not be discredited. (2 Corinthians 6:3)*

***Pursue Integrity***

*I know, my God, that you test the heart and are pleased with integrity. All these things I have given willingly and with honest intent. (1 Chronicles 29:17)*

- *in personal character.*

Exalt Christ, not self. Be honest, not exaggerating or over-promising; peace-loving, not contentious; patient, not volatile; diligent, not slothful. Avoid and, when necessary, report conflicts of interest and seek counsel.

- *in personal care.*

Care for the spiritual, mental, emotional and physical dimensions of your person, for *"your bodies are temples of the Holy Spirit"* (1 Corinthians 6:19).

- *in preaching and teaching.*

Interpret the Bible accurately and apply it discerningly: *"In your teaching show integrity, seriousness and soundness of speech that cannot be condemned"* (Titus 2:7-8). Speak the truth in love. Give due credit when using the words or ideas of others.

### Be Trustworthy

*It is required that those who have been given a trust must prove faithful. (1 Corinthians 4:2)*

- *in leadership.*

Model the trustworthiness of God in leadership to encourage and develop trustworthiness in others. Use power and influence prudently and humbly. Foster loyalty. Demonstrate a commitment to the well-being of the entire congregation. Keep promises. Respond sensitively and appropriately to ministry requests and needs: *"Whoever can be trusted with very little can also be trusted with much, and whoever is dishonest with very little will also be dishonest with much"* (Luke 16:10).

- *with information.*

Guard confidences carefully. Inform a person in advance, if possible, when an admission is about to be made that might legally require the disclosure of that information. Communicate truthfully and discreetly when asked about individuals with destructive or sinful behavior patterns. Tell the truth, or remain discreetly silent: *"A gossip betrays a confidence, but a trustworthy person keeps a secret"* (Proverbs 11:13).

- *with resources.*

Be honest and prudent in regard to personal and ministry resources. Refuse gifts that could compromise ministry. Ensure that all designated gifts are used for their intended purpose: *"If you have not been trustworthy in handling worldly wealth, who will trust you with true riches?"* (Luke 16:11).

### Seek Purity

*Don't let anyone look down on you because you are young, but set an example for the believers in speech, in conduct, in love, in faith and in purity. (1 Timothy 4:12)*

- *in maintaining sexual purity.*

Avoid sinful sexual behavior and inappropriate involvement. Resist temptation: *"Among you there must not be even a hint of sexual immorality"* (Ephesians 5:3a).

- *in spiritual formation.*

Earnestly seek the help of the Holy Spirit for guidance and spiritual growth. Be faithful to maintain a heart of devotion to the Lord. Be consistent and intentional in prayer and scriptural study: *"Take captive every thought to make it obedient to Christ"* (2 Corinthians 10:5).

- *in theology.*

Study the Bible regularly and carefully to understand its message, and embrace biblical doctrine. In forming theology, consider biblical teaching authoritative over all other sources.

- *in professional practice.*

Identify a minister/counselor who can provide personal counseling and advice when needed. Develop an awareness of personal needs and vulnerabilities. Avoid taking advantage of the vulnerabilities of others through exploitation or manipulation. Address the misconduct of another clergy member directly or, if necessary, through appropriate persons to whom that member of the clergy may be accountable.

## Embrace Accountability

*Be shepherds of God's flock that is under your care, watching over them— not because you must, but because you are willing, as God wants you to be; not pursuing dishonest gain, but eager to serve;*

*not lording it over those entrusted to you, but being examples to the flock. (1 Peter 5:2-3)*

- *in finances.*

Promote accepted accounting practices and regular audits. Ensure that church funds are used for their intended ministry purposes.

- *in ministry responsibilities.*

Ensure clarity in authority structures, decision-making procedures, position descriptions, and grievance policies. Model accountability at the highest organizational levels.

- *in a denomination or a ministry organization.*

Ensure compliance with denominational standards and expectations, including regular reports.

### Facilitate Fairness

*Believers in our glorious Lord Jesus Christ must not show favoritism. Suppose a man comes into your meeting wearing a gold ring and fine clothes, and a poor man in filthy old clothes also comes in. If you show special attention to the man wearing fine clothes and say, "Here's a good seat for you," but say to the poor man, "You stand there" or "Sit on the floor by my feet," have you not discriminated among yourselves and become judges with evil thoughts? (James 2:1-4)*

- *with staff.* Follow approved church and denomination practices in staff selection processes. Advocate for equitable pay and benefits for staff. Provide regular staff team building, affirmation, training, evaluation, and feedback. Be honest with staff regarding areas to celebrate and those needing improvement.

- *with parishioners.* Ensure appropriate access to staff by parishioners. Preach and teach to meet the needs of the entire congregation. Assume responsibility for congregational health. When asked for help beyond personal competence, refer others to those with requisite expertise.

- *with the community.* Build God's Kingdom in cooperation, not competition, with other local ministries. Provide Christian ministries to the public as possible. Encourage good citizenship.

- *with a prior congregation.* Do not recruit parishioners from a previous church without permission from the pastor. Avoid interfering in the ministry of a previous congregation.

As a minister of the Gospel, I commit to abide by the above Code of Ethics.

*Signature* _____

*Date*_____

*Printed Name*_____

*(By permission of **www.naecodeofethics.com**[1] )*

---

1.      http://www.naecodeofethics.com

# Appendix 5 The Integrity Pledge

In early 2021, the Desmond Tutu Centre for Leadership put forward a personalized pledge that was presented for "revival and moral regeneration" in a media article called *Goodbye Zondo, Hello Holiness*. It proposed something new - The Integrity Pledge - as a road-map out of corruption after the closure of the Zondo Commission.

- I will stop lying
- I will stop denying the obvious (that is, lying to myself)
- I will stop exaggerating, gossiping and slandering others
- I will stop stealing
- I will stop drinking excessively
- I will stop the womanizing (or the seduction)
- I will stop using foul language
- I will stop telling dirty jokes and ethnic jokes
- I will stop paying bribes and kick-backs
- I will stop taking bribes and kick-backs
- I will stop wasting non-renewable resources
- I will stop discriminating by race or by gender
- I will stop bullying (or beating)
- I will stop gaslighting, blame-shifting
- I will stop littering
- I will stop hoarding
- I will stop coveting what is not mine
- I will stop speeding
- I will stop covering up crimes
- I will stop condemning others
- I will stop over-indulging
- I will stop evading payment of taxes and debt

# About the Publisher

Mbokodo Publishers is your choice service provider and partner in the publishing business. We make your business our business in order to understand your needs, tastes and challenges better so we could provide you with the most efficient services imaginable.

Our professional and committed staff and personnel are always ready to assist you whenever you contact us. So drop us an email or simply call or visit our offices and this could be the beginning of a positive change in your life!

We look forward to being of ultimate assistance to you our dear prospective clients. For more information with regards to our offered products and services, please email us, mbokodopublishers@gmail.com

We look forward to hearing from you soon. God bless you!

Regards,

Publisher